Innovations in Information Retrieval

perspectives for theory and practice

Innovations in Information Retrieval

perspectives for theory and practice

Edited by

Allen Foster and Pauline Rafferty

facet publishing

Published by Facet Publishing,
7 Ridgmount Street, London WC1E 7AE
www.facetpublishing.co.uk

Facet Publishing is wholly owned by CILIP: the Chartered Institute of
Library and Information Professionals.

British Library Cataloguing in Publication Data
A catalogue record for this book is available from the British Library.

ISBN 978-1-85604-697-8
First published 2011

Text printed on FSC accredited material.

Typeset from editors' files by Facet Publishing in 10/12 pt Book Antiqua
and Frutiger.
Printed and made in Great Britain by CPI Group (UK) Ltd, Croydon CR0
4YY.

Contents

Figures and tables

———————●■●———————

Figures

Table

Contributors

David Bawden is Professor of Information Science at City University, London. He has a first degree in organic chemistry (Liverpool University) and master's and doctoral degrees in information science (Sheffield University), and worked in research information services in the pharmaceutical industry before joining City in 1990. His academic interests include history and philosophy of the information sciences, information-related behaviour, knowledge organization, scientific information, digital literacy and academic–practitioner research collaboration. He is editor of *Journal of Documentation*, the leading European journal of library/information science, and a member of the board of EUCLID, the European Association for Library and Information Teaching and Research. He has long-standing interests in browsing and other informal ways of accessing information, and in information for creativity and innovation.

Allen Foster is a lecturer in the Department of Information Studies at Aberystwyth University. His teaching and research interests span the study of user and systems, with a focus on interdisciplinarity, information seeking, serendipity and information retrieval. Interests include modelling the interrelationships between these areas and the information architecture of Web X social technologies. He holds degrees in history and information management and a PhD in information behaviour (University of Sheffield). Before his current position he was involved in several research projects at the University of Sheffield for a number of years, looking at subjects such as uncertainty and computer-mediated communication, along with his doctoral work on interdisciplinarity and non-linear information behaviour.

Luanne Freund is Assistant Professor at the School of Library, Archival and Information Studies at the University of British Columbia, where she teaches

IX

courses in information retrieval and information sources and services. She received her PhD from the Faculty of Information at the University of Toronto. Her research interests include human information interaction and information retrieval, with a particular focus on the role of domains, tasks and digital genres.

Charlie Inskip worked in the music industry from 1984 to 2005, in public relations and artist management. He took a master's in library and information studies (Distinction) at City University London in 2005/6. His dissertation, focusing on the user information needs of the Vaughan Williams Memorial Library of the English Folk Dance and Song Society, was awarded the E. T. Bryant Memorial Prize by the International Association of Music Libraries. He was recently awarded a PhD for his AHRC-funded research, entitled 'Upbeat and Quirky, with a Bit of a Build', which investigates the communication processes, meaning making and information needs of creatives, primarily in the music, film and advertising industries, who are searching for music and using it to accompany moving images. Charlie works as a music analyst and lecturer and writes a regular column for CILIP's *Library and Information Update* magazine in an attempt to demystify music information retrieval issues and make them relevant for library professionals.

Richard Kopak is Senior Instructor at the School of Library, Archival and Information Studies at the University of British Columbia, where he teaches courses in information design. He received his PhD from the Faculty of Information at the University of Toronto. His research interests are in the area of human information interaction and information design, focusing on the use of information structure in guiding user navigation.

Heather L. O'Brien is Assistant Professor at the School of Library, Archival and Information Studies at the University of British Columbia, where she teaches information-seeking behaviour. She received her interdisciplinary PhD from Dalhousie University, Halifax, Nova Scotia. Her research centres around users' engagement with technology and frameworks for understanding and measuring user experience in different contexts.

Isabella Peters studied German linguistics, German literature and information science at Heinrich Heine University Düsseldorf and gained her PhD in information science at the same university. Since 2007 she has worked as researcher and lecturer in the Department of Information Science of the Heinrich-Heine-University. Her main research focuses on folksonomies and social software as tools for information retrieval and knowledge representation, the evaluation of user-generated content for relevance ranking and the use of social software in knowledge management and academic education.

Pauline Rafferty is a senior lecturer in the Department of Information Studies, Aberystwyth University. Her research and scholarly interests focus on the analysis, retrieval and indexing of cultural documentation, including the indexing of fiction, library classification theory and history, genre theory, and critical communication and information studies. She is also interested in structuralist and semiotic approaches to modelling culture as 'human sciences' and holds a PhD in critical theory and cultural studies. Before joining Aberystwyth in January 2007, Pauline taught in the Department of Information Science, City University, London, and in the School of Information Studies and Department of Media and Communication at the University of Central England, Birmingham. Before moving into teaching, Pauline worked in information research and media librarianship.

Aida Slavic is the editor-in-chief of the Universal Decimal Classification (UDC Consortium, The Hague) and is responsible for the development and the maintenance of the schema. She is also a visiting lecturer at the Department of Information Sciences at the University of Zagreb, Croatia, where she teaches indexing languages, knowledge organization and information retrieval. Aida Slavic has a doctorate in Library and Information Studies from University College London. Her research interests are in the areas of knowledge organization, the use of classification in resource discovery, and modelling and formatting of controlled vocabularies for their use in a networked environment, subject access and subject metadata. She is member of the Scientific Advisory Board of the International Society for Knowledge Organization and one of the founding members and secretary of the British chapter of the International Society for Knowledge Organization.

Mike Thelwall is Professor of Information Science and leader of the Statistical Cybermetrics Research Group at the University of Wolverhampton, UK. He is also Docent at Åbo Akademi University Department of Information Studies, and a research associate at the Oxford Internet Institute. Mike has developed a wide range of tools for gathering and analysing web data, including hyperlink analysis, sentiment analysis and content analysis for Twitter, YouTube, MySpace, blogs and the web in general. His 300+ publications include 154 refereed journal articles, seven book chapters and two books, including *Introduction to Webometrics*; he is an associate editor of *Journal of the American Society for Information Science and Technology* and sits on six other editorial boards.

Anat Vernitski is responsible for bibliographic services at the UK Data Archive, covering collection management, thesauri development and cataloguers' training. Previously she worked in academic, art and medical libraries, with a focus on classification and information skills training. Her academic background is in literature and languages; she has a PhD in Russian literature, and has taught at the University of Essex, University of Surrey and UCL, and also in adult education. She is the author of a number of academic articles on classification, Russian literature and culture, and émigré history.

Foreword

In a dynamic and information-rich world information retrieval (IR) research and developments are the order of the day, as can be seen from numerous books and articles that are appearing. Scholars and practitioners may note some of these in passing. Serious scholars and researchers may take a closer look. When one is overwhelmed with information and other responsibilities it is, however, often difficult to note the finer nuances and shifts in a field – apart from carrying out systematic literature reviews. It is also difficult to find time to reflect and to notice gaps in research and practice in the field.

Innovations in Information Retrieval: perspectives for theory and practice is thus a very timely reminder of the importance of the field and the impact of IR research and theory on information users and their productivity, creativity, innovation, learning and communication. It also serves as an alert to both scholars and practitioners on the issues that might easily slip by without being noticed. The contributing authors bring many issues of importance for theory and practice to the fore. My thoughts when reading the chapter manuscripts were: I need to read this a few more times to make sure I pick up all the interesting ideas for further research; I wonder what my postgraduate students doing a course on IR, information seeking and information organization would note; and I really hope that decision-makers in libraries and information services will carefully study the text to spot challenges for practice. Before elaborating on these, a few words on some of the more obvious contributions of *Innovations in Information Retrieval*:

- An expert team in the IR, information organization and information-seeking fields is contributing. The diversity of contributions, ranging from serendipity and creativity to music and fiction retrieval, searching on the web, folksonomies and social tagging, and semantic navigation, brings to the front the interrelated nature of the field and how different issues impact on each other. For the scholarly reader and student it might be a good exercise to work through the chapters and see how each chapter can link to the arguments on serendipity and creativity. How can we read between the lines and come up with new ideas and stimulation for the field?

- The extensive and excellent lists of sources consulted portray the development in the field and often latest publications; these serve as excellent points of departure for further research, and especially for students and novice researchers to the field.
- The full spectrum of retrieval, organization and seeking is covered, and linked to the challenges that must be noted by scholars as well as practitioners.

Innovations in Information Retrieval is a welcome addition to a spectrum of monographs appearing in the field, which could serve graduate students, scholars, researchers and practitioners well in stimulating thoughts on gaps in research and practice, e.g. taking a multi-disciplinary approach to address issues of relevance, emotion and the importance of the user in music IR and turning it into an academic discipline. The value of webometric approaches to the evaluation of search engines and new ideas for research is explored. In addition, semantic navigation and digital information interaction with objects is addressed. The focus is on looking for solutions that can contribute to semantic navigation, namely genre, linking, annotation and user engagement. All these link well to a chapter on serendipity, creativity, innovation and styles of information seeking.

Taking a wider perspective on IR, *Innovations in Information Retrieval* lays the ground for IR being about more than the finding and location of relevant objects. It is about the need for IR researchers and practitioners to engage in active, purposeful learning and reflection and to make connections between research findings, ideas and practices, to work on the gaps and to contribute to the design of IR systems that can offer such opportunities and stimulation to their users. It is about the need for IR researchers and practitioners to emerge in the field and engage with its challenges to pave the way for innovative involvement. I therefore hope to see follow-up editions.

Professor Ina Fourie

Department of Information Science, University of Pretoria, South Africa

Introduction

————•●•————

Allen Foster and Pauline Rafferty

This is a book about research fronts in information retrieval and information organizations. As teachers of information retrieval and researchers in the field, we felt that a book specifically intended to inform and inspire Master's-level students who might be looking to develop their dissertation topics, or indeed to develop PhD proposals, would be useful and interesting We thought that this should be an edited and peer-reviewed book in which academics in information retrieval would be invited to write about the issues and topics that they think are of current interest and that they find engaging. This book, then, is intended to complement the information retrieval textbooks that are already in the market. The focus of this book is to introduce students to the broader information retrieval debates, theories and issues. To this end, contributors have been encouraged to highlight the 'hot' research ideas in their specialist area.

For many years the theory and practice of knowledge organization remained the preserve of information scientists and library professionals. The ubiquity and accessibility of the internet has changed this: no longer the sole concern of the library and information science (LIS) community, knowledge organization has caught the interest of computer scientists, semantic web developers and knowledge managers working in a wide range of organizations involved in the creation, storage, retrieval and dissemination of information, in particular, digital information. While traditional subject-oriented knowledge organization tools have been created and developed from within scholarly domains, so that the underlying concern has been to map 'knowledge' for academic purposes (e.g. DDC, LC, A&AT, Iconclass), contemporary subject-oriented knowledge organization tools are often driven by commercial, process and product-driven purposes.

The advent of new information retrieval technologies and approaches to storage and retrieval provides communities with previously unheard-of opportunities for mass documentation, digitization and the recording of cultural artefacts. A number of the contributors to this book focus in a variety of ways on issues relating to mass information retrieval in a digital age. In generating information retrieval for the public to contribute, describe and share, particular issues arise as to how shared meanings, quality of interpretation, indexing and tagging are accomplished. Related topics, such as generic categorization, semantic interoperability, dialogic semiotic interaction, once perhaps considered the preserve of other disciplines (linguistics, psychology, computer science), are increasingly of interest to the retrieval theorist and practitioner. Retrieval research includes speculation about what kinds of innovations and future directions are emerging (manual or automatic).

Typically, complex media have been at the forefront of techniques for metadata creation, management of collections and the issues new technologies bring to practical solutions and research explorations of information retrieval. Included in the book are chapters that explore music information retrieval and fiction retrieval, topics of interest in and of themselves, but also of interest because they bring into relief issues that impact on other kinds of documentation. Social tagging was the impossible and unbelievable extra dimension ten years ago. Interaction at the information-user level was not technologically, nor, from a professional indexer's point of view, desirable. With social networking tools, shared resources and online profiles, networked digital culture has driven forward information retrieval to include complex tagging experiments, user contributions and the development of folksonomies. The real questions for the future reflect on ways of understanding the social tagging contribution to information retrieval practice, managing the ends of social tagging if it is a fad and the creation of usable enhancements to social tagging to support organizational information retrieval. Traditional classification and the development of ontologies still play a significant role in information retrieval, even as user-based indexing is being developed; indeed theorists seem increasingly to take the view that the future of information retrieval systems will lie in the development of hybrid systems that include both formal and informal retrieval tools – the social semantic web.

It is an exciting time for information retrieval. There are many opportunities for the development of interesting projects covering a broad range of topics through a variety of research frameworks and methodologies. We hope that the authors and chapters we have brought together in this book will go some way towards inspiring the next generation to take up the challenges.

Outline of the book

If information retrieval is about bringing order and allowing successful storage and retrieval, then anything that challenges this basic idea seems bound to also be a rich source of questions. There can be no finer way to raise questions and ideas than by looking at the study of serendipity and browsing; both have been portrayed as the opposite of good practice at points in history and have tantalized readers, librarians and others with their seeming randomness and lack of structure. In the first chapter, 'Encountering on the road to Serendip?', David Bawden considers the continuing relevance of the ideas of browsing, serendipity, information encountering and literature discovery in the context of the modern information retrieval environment of the early 21st century, though its scope extends to the ideas in the broader contexts of information seeking and information-related behaviour. The central focus is on the question of how the concepts of browsing, serendipity and related ideas have changed in the new information retrieval environment of the web, and whether indeed they are still meaningful concepts. Challenging questions that span user interaction, information behaviour, and information storage and retrieval are explored. In her chapter 'Classification Revisited: a web of knowledge', Aida Slavic presents an overview of faceted classification research, which leads to a consideration of classification for computers in relation to a range of current issues such as web-ontology standards and folksonomies.

The focus of the book changes as the specialist areas of fiction retrieval and music retrieval are explored. In 'Approaches to Fiction Retrieval Research: from theory to practice?' by Anat Vernitski and Pauline Rafferty, a consideration of fiction retrieval research and initiatives provides an overview of some of the approaches that have been developed, including Pejtersen's 'Bookhouse' (1989) and whichbook.net. Key issues relating to intertextuality and generic categorization are considered and, in particular, two recent approaches to fiction retrieval that have made use of these theoretical concepts are described.

The work of Charlie Inskip in 'Music information retrieval research' continues the specialist focus. His chapter examines how the special nature of music impacts on the retrieval of digital audio and provides a critical overview of developments in the area of music information retrieval. Important musical facets are introduced and discussed in relation to the communication of musical meaning, which leads to an analysis of various metadata schemas. The importance of the music user as both a key source of research data and the ultimate participant of the musical communication process is discussed and existing approaches to the evaluation of music retrieval tools and systems are presented and considered.

The subject of information retrieval and its relationship to new approaches is discussed first by Isabella Peters in the chapter 'Folksonomies, Social Tagging and Information Retrieval'. Isabella Peters uses her chapter to investigate how far folksonomies meet the demands of 'social search'. Another section is dedicated to the relation between information retrieval and knowledge representation (Peters and Stock, 2010), in order to stress the necessity of indexing measures for information retrieval. Since the area of 'information retrieval' comprises the searching and finding of information in a very general way, and since there are many research paths for finding information (e.g. searching, browsing, retrieving, recommender systems or tag clouds), the chapter addresses these first and then discusses the importance of relevance ranking in folksonomy-based systems. Building on this, attention is drawn to the particularities of folksonomies in information retrieval and an outlook on further research areas is given.

Richard Kopak, Luanne Freund and Heather L. O'Brien use their chapter, 'Digital Information Interaction as Semantic Navigation', to explore a relatively recent and exciting development for retrieval research. Their focus is on the research area of digital information interaction, which emphasizes searchers' direct engagement with and manipulation of information objects as they search and browse through digital information environments. This is an area of active research that has opened up in recent years as information retrieval research has expanded its focus from the mechanics of retrieval (i.e. indexing, data structures and retrieval algorithms), to include a broader 'retrieval in context' perspective that takes into account the whole system, the affective, cognitive and physical attributes of users, and the environment in which searching takes place (Ingwersen and Järvelin, 2005).

Mike Thelwall explores webometrics in his chapter, 'Assessing Web Search Engines: a webometric approach'. This chapter introduces a range of webometric measurements and illustrates them with case studies of Google, Bing and Yahoo! This is a very fertile area for simple and complex new investigations into search engine results. The chapter begins with an overview, and the remainder of the chapter covers three separate categories: longitudinal studies of changes in results over time; internal consistency investigations of the differences between the results apparently known by a search engine and those it reports; and experiments into search engine coverage bias.

References

Ingwersen, P. and Järvelin, K. (2005) *The Turn: integration of information seeking and retrieval in context*, vol. 18, Springer.

Pejtersen, A. M. (1989) The 'Bookhouse': an icon based database system for fiction retrieval in public libraries. In Clausen, H. (ed.), *Information and Innovation: proceedings of the seventh Nordic conference for information and documentation*, Denmark: Arhus University, 165–78.

Peters, I. and Stock, W. G. (2010) 'Power Tags' in Information Retrieval, *Library Hi Tech*, **28** (1), 81–93.

Whichbook.net, www.whichbook.net/.

1

Encountering on the road to Serendip? Browsing in new information environments

David Bawden

Introduction

This chapter considers the continuing relevance of the ideas of browsing, serendipity, information encountering and literature discovery in the context of the information retrieval (IR) environment of 2010, though its scope extends to the ideas in the broader contexts of information seeking and information-related behaviour. It is based around a selective review of the literature since 1990 and reflection and speculation on the results. The central focus is on questions of how the concept of browsing, serendipity and related ideas have changed in the new IR environment of the web and whether, indeed, they are still meaningful concepts.

By the early 1990s, computerized retrieval was well established in practice and much investigated academically, but the internet was not widely used and the web was not developed. Browsing was a ubiquitous way of finding information, regarded as reasonably well understood. The literature on browsing, serendipity, creative use of information and associated topics up to that point has been thoroughly reviewed (Bawden, 1993a; Chang and Rice, 1993) and this older material will not be systematically covered in this chapter. More recent reviews and literature summaries are provided by Rice, McCreadie and Chang (2001), Foster and Ford (2003), Bates (2007), McBirnie (2008), Anderson (2010), Makri and Warwick (2010), Nutefall and Ryder (2010) and Case (2007), who analyses the concept of browsing and gives numerous examples of studies where its importance as a behaviour has been shown.

Browsing, as a concept, did not necessarily have a positive image among information specialists. I can recall being introduced, while studying for my master's degree, to the views of some senior practitioners who held that if users of a library were found to be browsing to any great extent, then this was a reflection on the library and its staff. Either its catalogues and indexes were inadequate, or the users had not been properly instructed in their use. Dr Urquhart, a luminary of the British library world at the time, expressed this view well: 'Browsing is no doubt a useful activity for an undergraduate who does not know what he wants but who must have a book immediately. Is it really a sensible activity in a research library? Is the browsing habit but the survival of an ancient custom or does it survive owing to bibliographic laziness or ignorance?' (Urquhart, 1976, 9). It is only fair to say that this view was challenged at the time by several writers (Bawden, 1993a).

It was also held that browsing was something that one did, indeed could only do, in printed materials. Computer searching was good for finding specific information, but was ill-suited and too expensive to allow for a browsing approach.

All these ideas now seem rather quaintly old fashioned. Developments in retrieval systems have meant that searching is now so effective that it is unlikely than anyone would adopt a browsing approach simply because there was no other way to find the desired information. On the other hand, the availability of large quantities of essentially free information, particularly on the internet, has led to the emergence of some new forms of information behaviour, which are often thought of as browsing; as Nicholas et al. (2004, 36) comment of their studies of web users, 'Browsing, time and time again in our studies, has proved to be the main method of obtaining information.' With other forms of media, browsing seems also to have grown, rather than diminished, in importance: it has, for example, been called 'a central search tactic in image retrieval' (Westman, 2009, 74).

Since the early 1990s, the major development in the practice of IR has been the advent of web-based digital information and the ubiquity of the web search engine as the retrieval tool. Web 2.0 tools and practices, such as social tagging, or folksonomy, and the widespread adoption of social media have had a 'second wave' impact on information seeking and retrieval, including browsing (De Meo et al., 2009). They have greatly expanded the amount of searching for information and simply 'coming across it' that takes place. The majority of this is clearly much more informal and more unstructured than heretofore and it may be reasonable to categorize much of it, roughly, as browsing. Indeed access to the web is invariably through a piece of software termed a browser. But does this mean that browsing and encountering cease to be distinct or useful specific concepts; are we, in fact, all browsers now? To answer this question, we need to consider the wider contexts of information seeking and information-related behaviour.

Studies of web behaviour have shown unusual and previously unsuspected patterns of use (Nicholas et al., 2004; Heinström, 2005), and the concepts of 'information encountering' (Erdelez, 2004) and 'serendipitous seeking' (Foster and Ford, 2003) have been put forward. Although clearly browsing of a kind, they are rather different from the concept as it was understood 20 years ago.

The link between browsing and the use of information systems and services for stimulating innovation and creativity has long been recognized, and for an obvious reason. Search implies, in a way that browsing does not, a clearly defined idea or concept in mind, with information being sought to confirm, support or refute it, or to set it in context. It cannot, as browsing has always been held to do, throw up new ideas or new connections between ideas, which are the *sine qua non* of creativity and innovation.

The idea that IR systems could be relevant as stimuli and aids to creativity had been put forward well before our starting point of the early 1990s; see reviews by Bawden (1986) and Swanson (1990). It has been considered since, again in the new context of a largely digital information environment; see, for example, Schneiderman (2001), Eaglestone et al. (2007) and Swanson, Smalheiser and Torvik (2006). It seems reasonable, therefore, to consider these developments alongside those for browsing, encountering and serendipitous information.

This chapter deals with the central question of how the concept of browsing and the related ideas noted above have changed in the new IR environment of the web, and to what extent they are still meaningful concepts. It is based on a selective review of a very wide literature since 1990, focusing on contributions from information science rather than the other disciplines that have an interest in these topics.

Seven more specific questions are considered:

- Is browsing still a meaningful description of a style of IR and a type of information behaviour?
- How do the newer forms of information behaviour in web environments relate to traditional ideas of browsing?
- How do newer forms of IR system enable serendipity, information encountering, literature discovery and creativity stimulation, compared with earlier forms?
- Do tagging, folksonomy and other Web 2.0 and social media influences on information seeking promote browsing, and how may they best be applied?
- How can we best understand, explain and categorize browsing in the current IR environment?
- Can we helpfully identify individual 'information styles' associated with browsing, encountering and serendipity, and creativity?
- How can IR systems best support browsing, encountering and creativity?

Browsing

Browsing has generally been distinguished from searching by having a less well-defined end-point, in terms of the information being sought, and a less structured approach to finding items of interest and relevance. Where searching is formal and analytical, browsing is informal and heuristic (Marchionini, 1995).

While it seems clear what browsing is, in practice, precise definitions are few and not generally agreed, perhaps because the term can cover a variety of activities and purposes. Chu (2010) describes it as 'seeking and selecting information by skimming, scanning and other similar activities'. Cove and Walsh (1988) gave perhaps the best general explanation, saying simply that it is 'the art of not knowing what you want until you find it'. The finding may be in itself a Eureka moment, again emphasizing the link between browsing and innovation/creativity.

Equally, a number of terms are used to mean browsing and similar activities. A nice example of this is the index entry from Case (2007, 415):

Browsing
see also Discovering, Encountering, Foraging, Grazing, Navigating, Scanning, Zapping

It has been usual to distinguish between various forms of browsing. *Active* browsing, for example, where some definite information was sought, may be distinguished from *passive* browsing, a general scanning with no particular end in mind. A distinction has also often been made between *directed, semi-directed* and *undirected* browsing, again depending on the extent to which some defined information is being sought through browsing, as against a situation of simply scanning sources in the hope of noticing something interesting. This latter categorization was first made in one of the earliest reviews of browsing in the literature (Herner, 1970) and was revised by Vickery (1977) as *purposive, semi-purposive* and *capricious*. A somewhat similar categorization of browsing as *systematic, exploratory* and *casual* has been made by Marchionini (1995) and as *search/directed, general* purpose and *serendipitous/random* (Cove and Walsh, 1987; Catledge and Pitkow, 1995). A number of rather similar categorizations, generally three-way, have been proposed (Bawden, 1993a).

A variation was introduced by Bates (1986), who divided information-seeking behaviour by two criteria – active/passive and directed/undirected – giving a four-way categorization, with the active-directed category corresponding to conventional IR. Bates regarded the active-undirected category as browsing – approximating the purposive form of other categorizations – but not the two passive categories, as no active attempt was being made to find information. It seems more realistic to regard Bates's passive-directed and passive-undirected as being other forms of browsing, akin to what would later be termed encountering. More recently, Bates (2007) has analysed studies of browsing to suggest that it typically has a four-stage nature: glimpsing a 'field of vision'; selecting an object within it; examining the object; acquiring or abandoning it.

It seems that, looking beneath the variant terminology, a fairly consistent understanding of different forms of browsing had emerged by the early 1990s and that later work has not substantially revised it. The only major theoretical extension has been an analysis presented in a 1995 thesis and reported by Chang (2005), which identified nine patterns of browsing within five general purposes. From outside the information sciences, the 'information foraging' model has gained some interest as relevant to browsing approaches (Pirolli, 2007; Pirolli and Card, 1999; Cronin and Hert, 1995; Jacoby, 2005).

Browsing has, arguably, been given greater credibility by its being included as a component of a number of models of information-seeking behaviour, although, as Foster and Ford (2003) point out, these do not usually extend to unstructured serendipitous encountering. Examples are:

- Wilson's (1999, 2005) model, which includes *passive attention* and *passive search* as components
- Ellis's (1989, 2005) model, which has *browsing* (understood as semi-directed searching) as one component
- Foster's (2004, 2005a, 2005b) non-linear model, which has a process of opening, including activities of *browsing* and *serendipity*
- McKenzie's (2003) model of information practices in everyday-life information seeking, which involves *active scanning* (including semi-directed browsing) and *non-directed monitoring* (serendipitous encountering)
- Chu's (2009) analysis of environmental scanning, which includes *undirected viewing* as one of four modes, involving the scanning of large amounts of information from many and varied sources of information
- Makri and Warwick's (2010) model for 'information for inspiration', which, in addition to *browsing*, includes *exploration* ('finding information either without a predefined goal or to address a vaguely-defined goal').

Further examples are noted by Yuan and Belkin (2010).

Makri and Warwick (2010) also relate stages or processes in information-behaviour models to a 'creativity framework' with associated information tasks (Schneiderman, 2001). The four stages of this framework are:

- collect – essentially the use of conventional information systems, with browsing and visualizing emphasized
- relate – communicating with peers and mentors

- create – which may include serendipitous association of concepts and reflective reviewing of information
- donate – communication of insights gained.

As noted above, browsing – once largely a method of finding information in printed sources which had to be adopted because of the lack of adequate indexes and other tools to assist searching – has not disappeared in the digital environment, despite advances in search functionality. Its continuing popularity is unsurprising, since, as Chu (2010) points out, it is a natural and simple way of finding information, less intellectually demanding than alternatives and needing little in the way of training and practice.

Furthermore, browsing can achieve things which alternative tactics cannot. There are numerous purposes for browsing, some of which are enumerated by Marchionini (1995) and Chu (2010). They include:

- finding information in a context where browsing is the only feasible method
- finding information on topics which are not clearly defined or which are hard to specify exactly, i.e. where the information need is broad and poorly specified
- getting an overview or sample of the information in a collection
- finding items which are similar to, or dissimilar from, those which one has identified
- finding one's bearing in a subject of which one knows little
- selecting the 'right' information from a large collection of 'relevant' material
- looking for inspiration, new ideas, or just something interesting, i.e. allowing for serendipity.

Crucially, even in fully digital environments, browsing may lead to unexpected, serendipitous information discovery precisely because it is much more likely to lead to the finding of unanticipated material. It does this because of its unstructured nature, compared with conventional search, and hence its openness to material of very varied – at the extreme, random – nature.

In addition to categorization by purpose – *why* people browse – there have been categorizations of browsing tactics – *how* browsing is done.

I put forward the idea, in a review more than 15 years ago, that browsing, in practice, usually meant one of three distinct things, though all have been called browsing (Bawden, 1993a):

- finding items similar to one or more items already known, where the

nature of the similarity remains fuzzily defined
- following a predefined categorization, usually hierarchal, through an information space, to identify interesting items
- obtaining an overview of the variation of items in an information space, so as to identify interesting areas of that space.

Marchionini (1995) distinguishes four browsing strategies:

- scanning – looking sequentially through lists of information
- observing – looking in an unstructured way at whatever information presents itself
- navigating – following routes provided by the system
- monitoring – a multi-tasking approach, examining various information sources simultaneously.

Chang's (2005) model presents nine *patterns of browsing* within five *general themes*:

- looking for a specific item
  - situational browsing
  - opportunistic browsing
- looking for things with common characteristics
  - systematic browsing
  - evaluative browsing
  - focus browsing
- keeping up to date
  - monitoring browsing
- learning or finding out
  - indicative browsing
  - preparatory browsing
- goal free
  - invitational browsing.

While all of these strategies and patterns could, in principle, be used in a print-on-paper environment, they have been supported and enhanced by features of digital information systems. These are reviewed by Kowalski (1997), Ruthven (2008) and Chu (2010), and only a few additional example references are given below. These features include:

- ranked results lists and other 'browsable' lists (Jacso, 2005; Hoare and Sorensen, 2005)

- clustering of results (Crestani and Wu, 2006)
- faceted browsing (Perugini, 2010; Fagan, 2010)
- automatic classification and categorization (Tang, 2007; Golub and Lykke, 2009)
- hyperlinks (Mobrand and Spyridakis, 2007)
- directory and classification structures (Perugini, 2010; Koch, Golub and Ardo, 2006)
- highlighting of information elements (Toms, 2002)
- graphical visualization of information (Hoare and Sorensen, 2005; Westerman, Collins and Cribbin, 2005)
- support of integrated searching and browsing (Tang, 2007).

These seem, on the whole, to support the more purposive/directed styles of browsing and navigation, rather than serendipitous/undirected styles.

We should also mention developments in the handling of chemical information. With the advantage of dealing with complete and unambiguous representations of chemical structures, techniques were developed for calculating similarity and dissimilarity between substances and diversity of substance collections (Bawden, 1988, 1993b, Willett, 2008, 2009). These methods are transferable to other forms of information (Wade, Willett and Bawden, 1989; Willett, 2000) and are highly relevant to the browsing process, where what is often wanted is items similar to a given, or dissimilar from it within constraints, or representative items from a collection, spanning its diversity as much as possible.

The development of folksonomies and social tagging, as a complement or alternative both to conventional indexing by controlled vocabularies and to full-text searching, has the potential to improve browsability and also to offer a better chance of serendipitous discovery because of the multiple, often unconventional, perspectives offered (Peters, 2009, ch. 4). Systems relying on social tagging often have interfaces offering specific support for exploratory searching and browsing (Shiri, 2009). However, the sheer volume and diversity of tags can be a problem, and faceting and clustering of tags can aid the browsing process (De Meo et al., 2009; Ding et al., 2009; Spiteri, 2010).

Despite the current overwhelming emphasis on digital materials, support for browsing is still an important feature of printed collections, as witness the appeals by Kirk (2010) for 'browsing collections' in academic libraries and by Hoeflich (2007) for the support of serendipity in legal libraries and archives, the argument of Boyd (2000) for the serendipity-provoking arrangement of physical collections, and the success of the London Library's 'idiosyncratic' classification schema 'based firmly on the principle of serendipity' (Flood, 2007, 51).

Browsing therefore still seems to be a realistic description of an important, and arguably increasingly important, way of finding information that may be categorized and examined. However, the findings of studies of web behaviour, based mainly on detailed analysis of web-logs combined with more traditional survey methods showing exactly what users are doing, shows a somewhat different picture. Although some aspects of these behaviours may be described as browsing, it is a rather different style of browsing from that discussed above. Nicholas et al. (2004) identified 'bouncing' and 'flicking', a very rapid movement from site to site without any in-depth examination of their content, in contrast to other search styles involving, for example, repeated returning to the same pages or checking of the same information on different sites. Heinström (2005) identified 'fast surfing', a similar style of rapid movement from site to site with only limited examination of information possible, and 'broad scanning', a wide-ranging and generally unstructured examination of a variety of material (discussed further below), by contrast with styles such as 'deep diving', in-depth investigation of a few resources. These results suggest that new forms of browsing have developed to deal with the web environment and that browsing is an important, though not universal, approach.

Encountering and serendipity

Browsing, as discussed above, may be used in a wide spectrum of information seeking, in different ways and for different purposes. One aspect or style of browsing is particularly associated with serendipitous or accidental information access: the random, exploratory, passive scanning aspect, which is commonly associated with the use of information to stimulate innovation and creativity. Indeed, the two things – browsing and creative use of information – have, for many years, often been treated as synonymous (Bawden, 1986). Regarded in earlier years as something of a mystical art, inaccessible to analysis, this style of information acquisition has been examined recently from a variety of viewpoints. These have been as much concerned with the wider information-related behaviour context as with the more specific contexts of information seeking and IR.

The most thorough analysis has taken the form of the concept of 'information encountering', introduced by Erdelez (1997, 1999, 2004, 2005). This alludes to the finding of useful information by accident, also termed serendipitous information acquisition, and to means employed by information users to maximize the chance of this. On an initial basis of interview and questionnaire studies with university students, Erdelez identified four categories of information user, depending on the extent to which they relied on accidental encounters to satisfy their information needs: non-encounterers, occasional encounterers, encounterers and super-encounterers. For the last group, this was the preferred means of finding information and they took active steps to promote it, going well beyond use of formal information systems, for example, systematically examining reading materials left behind by others. They were also typically active in identifying encountered information of use to others and communicating it to them, strongly emphasizing the personalized nature of this kind of information interaction (Erdelez and Rioux, 2000).

The idea has been developed by Erdelez (2005) into a more detailed model of accidental encountering of interesting information during some other task, involving steps of noticing, stopping, examining, capturing and returning. She also positions it within a more general category of 'opportunistic acquisition of information', allowing for the possibility that encountering is not the only mechanism for such acquisition.

Interestingly, the negative image of browsing mentioned above has persisted, to an extent, to the present day, since Erdelez (1999) comments that super-encounterers were unwilling to speak about it, as they felt theirs was not an 'approved' method of finding information and they might even be ridiculed for admitting they relied on it. Echoing the points made above about the value of printed materials for browsing, many super-encounterers preferred these resources, and in particular avoided the internet as a source. For others who rely less on encountering, the internet is a primary environment for encountering information, along with libraries and bookshops.

This encountering idea has been used in other studies; Pálsdóttir (2010), for example, identifies four categories of information-seeking behaviour in a large-scale study of the ways in which Icelanders find information on health and lifestyle and finds encountering to occur in all of them, but in active or passive ways in different categories. In a small-scale study of health-information seeking among Latino immigrants to the USA, Courtright (2005) found that serendipitous encountering figured strongly in information interactions with positive outcomes; these were generally personal interactions. Essentially the same phenomenon, though termed 'incidental information acquisition', was identified in a study of the everyday-life information seeking of older people (Williamson, 1998). Ross (1999) described 'finding without seeking', whereby those who read for pleasure encountered information that made a significant difference to their lives – a good example of encountering in unconventional sources. Foster and Ford (2003) found that serendipity was widely experienced in the information behaviour of inter-disciplinary academic researchers. Makri and Warwick (2010) found that serendipitous encountering was a significant factor in the information behaviour of architecture students, particularly when seeking inspiration and often in the context of examining images.

Encountering also seems rather similar to the idea of 'broad scanning', noted above as a style of information behaviour identified by Heinström, as an aspect emerging from a factor analysis of detailed data on information behaviour. This was defined as 'a search pattern characterized by wide and thorough information seeking . . . [practitioners] sought information from many different sources, retrieved information by chance and found it easy to judge information critically' (Heinström, 2005, 237). Accidental information acquisition was much more common in this style than in others.

We should also mention a rather different form of creative use of information, quite distinct from browsing and encountering. This is the specific and formal use of a procedure or algorithm for 'information discovery', finding analogies and relations within information collections, which had not been previously recognized; for a thorough review, see Kostoff et al. (2009). This idea has been mainly promoted and developed for the medical information domain (Swanson, 1990), with a variety of systems developed to identify unappreciated ideas implicit in the literature, generally on the basis of joint occurrence of thesaurus terms in metadata records; see, for example Swanson and Smalheiser (1999), Weeber et al. (2001), Swanson, Smalheiser and Torvik (2006) and Petric et al. (2009). This is a very different concept, in practice if not in principle, from the browsing ideas discussed above, showing the variety of solutions necessary for this diverse area.

The personal factor

A prevalent theme in writings on information for creativity has been the extent to which this has a strongly personal and individual dimension. The kind of information needed, the way it is identified and the means used for browsing and encountering all differ considerably between individuals; some examples have been given above. This is one specific example of the general finding that personality traits can make people more prone to serendipity (Merton and Barber, 2004).

This 'individual differences' aspect has been analysed more precisely in a number of studies of the relation between information-related behaviour and personality factors, learning styles and cognitive styles; for recent reviews, see Heinström (2010) and Bawden and Robinson (2010). A number of such studies have specifically investigated browsing and serendipitous approaches to information, finding links between preferences for such behaviours and ways of implementing them, and personality factors.

Graff (2005), for example, using Riding's Cognitive Styles Analysis (Riding and Rayner, 1998; Ford, 2000), found a distinction between the web-browsing strategies of verbalizer and imager style, the former using more pages set up in a hierarchical arrangement, the latter using more relationally linked pages.

Heinström (2006) has related a tendency for 'incidental information acquisition' to personality factors, showing it to be favoured by those with high motivation, an energetic personality and positive emotionality, and avoided those inclined to stress, insecurity and low motivation.

The same author (Heinström, 2010) has given a detailed analysis of many aspects of information behaviour in terms of the widely used 'five factor' model of personality (Wiggins, 1996), which considers five personality traits or dimensions: neuroticism, extroversion, openness, agreeableness and conscientiousness. A high level of openness, for example, might be expected to lead to a propensity for encountering and for creative use of information, and there is some evidence to support this. This was not established, however, in one study which specifically examined such factors (Heinström, 2006), suggesting that other factors may play a significant part. A high degree of extroversion, leading to an active and spontaneous style of information seeking, might be expected to lead to a large extent of incidental encountering, and this has been confirmed in one study (Heinström, 2006).

On the basis of such considerations, Heinström (2010) developed a fivefold categorization of 'information attitude'. Three of the attitudes involved a preference for some form of browsing:

- *invitational attitude*: an open personality with an intuitive searching style, leading to a high degree of serendipity
- *exploring attitude*: again an open personality, but relying more on a broad scanning style
- *passive attitude*: low on conscientiousness and relying on a fast surfing style of browsing to find the necessary information with the minimum of input.

The Honey–Mumford conception of learning styles (Honey and Mumford, 1986), which identifies four preferred styles – Activist, Pragmatist, Theorist and Reflector – is held to have a relation to information behaviour because of the strong links between learning and information acquisition (Bawden and Robinson, 2010). They have been used explicitly, as a surrogate information style, to plan training and personalized service delivery in a multinational company (Donnelly and Craddock, 2007). An 'information activist', with a Honey–Mumford activist style, might be expected to be an enthusiastic networker, keen to try many and diverse sources in a rather unstructured way.

Although many of the results of such studies are indicative rather than conclusive, we can see that it is feasible to define and identify information styles as they relate to browsing and creativity.

Serendipity systems?

Nearly 25 years ago, I suggested a number of desirable criteria for information systems focusing on the support of serendipitous information discovery (Bawden, 1986). Of course, innovation and creativity depend on the 'prepared mind', which will generally rely on the input from more conventional information systems. But there may be some specific features which can be recommended to meet this particular purpose. My suggestions at that time were:

- inclusion of peripheral and speculative material
- provision of interdisciplinary information
- representations of information to bring out analogies, patterns, exceptions etc.
- emphasis on browsing facilities
- encouragement of informal channels
- information geared to individual preferences and requirements
- direct involvement of the information user
- appropriate use of new information technologies
- an overall information-rich environment.

The last three have been effectively assured by technological developments in the intervening years; the rest I believe to be still valid and supported by more recent developments and studies.

Since then, there have been a relatively small number of studies specifically addressing this issue: these include those of Ford (1999), Schneiderman (2001), Eaglestone et al. (2007), Makri and Warwick (2010) and Anderson (2010). Many other studies have addressed these issues in part, as noted above.

So what would such a system be like?

First and foremost, it would have to be a personal system with a customizable interface and an adjustable balance between focus and diversity. We have noted above the strong element of individual and personal style in this area, and this must be catered for if systems are to be accepted and successful.

It would have to be based around promoting the possibility of serendipitous information discovery. But, as Ford (1999, 532 and 537) points out, 'such flashes of insight seem far removed from the focused and systematic search for information . . . there would seem to be a considerable mismatch between the element of serendipity that often characterizes creative thinking and what IR systems are essentially designed to deliver'. It is not clear, despite the various suggestions noted above, that we really know what such a system would look like. Some would say that it would look like the browsable shelves of a library of books: either a physical library or its virtual equivalent (see, for example, Beheshti, Large and Bialek, 1996).

As we have seen, browsing is frequently based on analysis of similarity and its converse, dissimilarity. As Ford (1999) points out, similarity recognition is also central to creative thinking, another link between browsing and creative use of information. Any system for these purposes would have to be based around similarity and dissimilarity assessments, in a deeper and more sophisticated way than the widely used probabilistic retrieval systems.

It has been suggested for many years that the kind of information that is most valuable in supporting creativity and innovation may be rather different from that needed for more usual purposes. I suggested some long while ago (Bawden, 1986) that four kinds of information were of most value: interdisciplinary, peripheral, speculative and that focusing on exceptions and inconsistencies.

This amounts to saying that relevance criteria should be relaxed or modified in systems focusing on this purpose, and this suggestion has received support in the literature. For example, Spink and Greisdorf (1997) found that it was partially relevant, rather than highly relevant, items which were most helpful in promoting new ideas, while Ford (1999) argued for a balance between relevance and diversity in support of creativity. Interestingly, Bodoff (2006) found that very different judgements about the relevance of an item were made by searchers who were browsing around an area, as compared with those who were carrying out a focused search, emphasizing the different kind of material valued by each.

Going even further, it has been suggested that random, or even incorrect, information may be valuable in provoking creativity. The former is catered for by undirected forms of browsing and has frequently appeared in internet search systems, seemingly as a 'fun' option rather than anything more serious. The latter is still beyond the pale for most information systems and services, though it is accepted as a brainstorming tool. (An intriguing fictional account of the value of providing deliberately incorrect information [Jones, 1971] was one of the – serendipitous – stimuli for my interest in this topic.)

A system of the kind we are envisaging would need novel search facilities, so distinct from the norm that we might not wish to call them 'search', or even 'browse', at all.

As long ago as 1979, Bates proposed a set of 17 'idea tactics' for searchers, to help generate new ideas and promote creativity. They include such heuristics as:

- *wander* – move among one's resources, being receptive to alternative sources and new search ideas which come into view
- *jolt* and *breach* – think laterally, redefine a problem completely differently, revise ideas of the boundaries of the area being considered

- *focus* and *dilate* – look at an issue or query more narrowly or more broadly
- *change* and *break* – alter an established search pattern, search in a very different way, try different sources etc.
- *notice* – watch for clues in information retrieved that may change one's view of the problem.

These clearly bear strong a relation to browsing approaches discussed earlier and typify the sorts of unconventional facilities needed if information systems are to support creativity.

Ford (1999) argued that such systems must respond to two general types of query: those which find a pattern of relationships, which will integrate seemingly disparate information, and those which find instances of a concept or relationship similar to a starting-point in a variety of contexts and subject areas. As Ford notes, this would need higher-order knowledge representations, in order to allow abstraction across different subjects and contexts and fuzzy matching, considerably beyond what is the norm.

Makri and Warwick (2010) give a detailed set of recommendations for 'creative' electronic resources, with features including: augmented searching; browsing by various criteria; supporting serendipity by integrating materials for diverse sources, categorized and shared in personal ways; and visualization techniques to show a rapid snapshot of diverse information. They emphasize the importance of browsing of visual material for serendipity and inspiration at least for some user groups, as do André et al. (2009). Yuan and Belkin (2010) have shown how a system may be designed to support specific information-seeking strategies, including scanning of resources and results.

To conclude this section, we might consider what basic set of facilities a system would have to offer in order to be regarded as adequate for this purpose. I suggest the following, based on the considerations presented above:

Show examples of what the system has
1   show a random document
    given: a statement of the content of the collection
2   show representatives of document clusters
    given: a statement of the content of the collection
    and: an option to select the number of clusters required.

Show the structure of what the system has
3   show an alphabetically ordered list of subject terms
    given: a statement of the content of the collection
    and: an option to choose the level of generality of the terms

4   show a classified list of subject terms
     given: a statement of the content of the collection.

Show what the system has, related to what I already know about
5   show a ordered list of documents in descending order of similarity to the
     input
     given: an initial specified document or query
6   show an ordered list of documents in descending order of dissimilarity to
     the input
     given: an initial specified document or query.

This requires that the system have:

• a collection of structured records, e.g. bibliographic records
• a field for indexing terms, these terms being taken from a vocabulary with
  a term hierarchy, i.e. a thesaurus or taxonomy
• a search function, to identify initial documents for functions 5 and 6 (from
  the above list)
• the capability to display documents indexed with terms selected from a
  list
• the capability to cluster documents, in such a way that the user can be
  offered alternative numbers of clusters.

This is a rather basic set of functions and abilities, with an arguably rather
uninteresting collection of material. It could be extended, based on the same
general functions, to allow for multiple types of materials and varying
representations, including those of higher abstraction.

Conclusion

This review has shown that increases in understanding of the issues and
developments in practice bring closer the possibility of information systems that
will be able to make direct and genuine contributions to innovation and
creativity.

But we should remember that the individual and idiosyncratic natures of the
use of information for innovation and creativity are likely to elude the best-
motivated attempts of system designers to cater for them in any formal sense.
Twenty-five years ago, a staff member of the then College of Librarianship
Wales related a telling anecdote in a letter to a newspaper (Roe, 1985):

One university lecturer has stated that he makes a practice of noting down the registration numbers of the cars parked outside the library, and consulting the books shelved at those numbers in the library. Rarely does he fail to find something of interest and instruction in this way. Information technology whiz-kids and the new librarians . . . ignore such quirks of human behaviour at their peril.

Building systems and services in the light of the considerations reviewed in this chapter should help whiz-kids and librarians alike to avoid this danger.

References

Anderson, T. D. (2010) Kickstarting Creativity: supporting the productive faces of uncertainty in information practice, *Information Research*, in press.

André, P., Cutrell, E., Tan, D. S. and Smith, G. (2009) Designing Novel Image Search Interfaces by Understanding Unique Characteristics and Usage: paper presented at *INTERACT 2000, Uppsala, Sweden, August 2009*, http://research.microsoft.com/en-us/um/people/desney/publications/interact2009-tendrils.pdf.

Bates, M. J. (1979) Idea Tactics, *Journal of the American Society for Information Science*, **30** (5), 280–9.

Bates, M. J. (1986) An Exploratory Paradigm for Online Information Retrieval. In Brookes, B. C. (ed.), *Intelligent Information Systems for the Information Society*, North-Holland.

Bates, M. J. (2007) What is Browsing – Really? A model drawing from behavioural science research, *Information Research*, **12** (4), Paper 330, http://InformationR.net/ir/12-4/paper330.html.

Bawden, D. (1986) Information Systems and the Stimulation of Creativity, *Journal of Information Science*, **12** (5), 203–16.

Bawden, D. (1988) Browsing and Clustering of Chemical Structures. In Warr, W. A. (ed.), *Chemical Structures; the international language of chemistry*, Springer Verlag, 145–50.

Bawden, D. (1993a) Browsing: theory and practice, *Perspectives in Information Management*, **3** (1) 71–85.

Bawden, D. (1993b) Molecular Dissimilarity in Chemical Information Systems. In Warr, W. A. (ed.), *Chemical Structures 2*, Springer Verlag, 383–8.

Bawden, D. and Robinson, L. (2010) Individual Differences in Information-related Behaviour: towards identifying information styles. In Spink, A. and Heinström, J. (eds), *New Directions in Information Behaviour*, Emerald, forthcoming.

Beheshti, J., Large, V. and Bialek, M. (1996) PACE: a browsable graphical interface, *Information Technology and Libraries*, **1594**, 231–40.

Bodoff, D. (2006) Relevance for Browsing, Relevance for Searching, *Journal of the*

American Society for Information Science and Technology, **57** (1), 69–86.

Boyd, B. (2000) Serendipity of the New, *Journal of Rare Books, Manuscripts and Cultural Heritage*, **1** (1), 36–7.

Case, D. O. (2007) *Looking for Information: a survey of research on information seeking, needs, and behavior*, 2nd edn, Academic Press.

Catledge, L. D. and Pitkow, J. E. (1995) Characterizing Browsing Strategies in the World-Wide Web, *Computer Networks and ISDN Systems*, **27** (6), 1065–73.

Chang, S.-J. (2005) Chang's Browsing. In Fisher, K. E., Erdelez, S. and McKechnie, L. E. F. (eds), *Theories of Information Behavior*, Information Today, 69–74.

Chang, S.-J. and Rice, R. E. (1993) Browsing: a multi-dimensional framework, *Annual Review of Information Science and Technology*, **28**, 231–76.

Chu, C. W. (2009) The Art of Scanning the Environment, *Bulletin of the American Society for Information Science*, **25** (3), available at www.asis.org/Bulletin/Feb-99/choo.html.

Chu, H. (2010) *Information Representation and Retrieval in the Digital Age* (2nd edn), Information Today.

Courtright, C. (2005) Health Information-seeking among Latino Newcomers: an exploratory study, *Information Research*, **10** (2), Paper 224, http://InformationR.net/ir/10-2/paper224.html.

Cove, J. F. and Walsh, B. C. (1987) Browsing as a Means of Online Text Retrieval, *Information Services and Use*, **7** (6), 183–8.

Cove, J. F. and Walsh, B. C. (1988) Online Text Retrieval via Browsing, *Information Processing and Management*, **24** (1), 31–7.

Crestani, F. and Wu, S. (2006) Testing the Cluster Hypothesis in Distributed Information Retrieval, *Information Processing and Management*, **42** (5), 1137–50.

Cronin, B. and Hert, C. A. (1995) Scholarly Foraging and Network Discovery Tools, *Journal of Documentation*, **51** (4), 388–403.

De Meo, P. et al. (2009) Exploitation of Semantic Relationships and Hierarchical Data Structures to Support a User in his Annotation and Browsing Activities in Folksonomies, *Information Systems*, **34** (6), 511–35.

Ding, Y. et al. (2009) Perspectives on Social Tagging, *Journal of the American Society for Information Science and Technology*, **60** (12), 2388–401.

Donnelly, A. and Craddock, C. (2007) Information Discovery Stir-fry: information literacy in the commercial sector. In Secker, J., Boden, D. and Price, G. (eds), *The Information Literacy Cookbook*, Chandos, 45–70.

Eaglestone, B. et al. (2007) Information Systems and Creativity: an empirical study, *Journal of Documentation*, **63** (4), 443–64.

Ellis, D. (1989) A Behavioural Approach to Information Retrieval System Design, *Journal of Documentation*, **45** (3), 171–212.

Ellis, D. (2005) Ellis's Model of Information-seeking Behaviour. In Fisher, K. E., Erdelez, S. and McKechnie, L. E. F. (eds), *Theories of Information Behavior*,

Information Today, 138–42.

Erdelez, S. (1997) Information Encountering: a conceptual framework for accidental information discovery. In Vakkari, P., Savolainen, R. and Dervin, B. (eds), *Information Seeking in Context: proceedings of the international conference on research in information needs, seeking and use in different contexts (August 1996, Tampere)*, Taylor Graham, 412–21.

Erdelez, S. (1999) Information Encountering: it's more than just bumping into information, *Bulletin of the American Society for Information Science*, **25** (3), www.asis.org/Bulletin/Feb-99/erdelez.html.

Erdelez, S. (2004) Investigation of Information Encountering in the Controlled Research Environment, *Information Processing and Management*, **40** (6), 1013–25.

Erdelez, S. (2005) Information Encountering. In Fisher, K. E., Erdelez, S. and McKechnie, L. E. F. (eds), Theories of Information Behaviour, *Information Today*, 179–84.

Erdelez, S. and Rioux, K. (2000) Sharing Information Encountered for Others on the Web, *New Review of Information Behaviour Research*, **1**, 219–33.

Fagan, J. C. (2010) Usability Studies of Faceted Browsing: a literature review, *Information Technology and Libraries*, **29** (2), 58–66.

Flood, G. (2007) The London Library: portrait of a lady, *Information Today*, **24** (1), 1, 51, 54.

Ford, N. (1999) Information Retrieval and Creativity: towards support for the original thinker, *Journal of Documentation*, **55** (5), 528–42.

Ford, N. (2000) Cognitive Styles and Virtual Environments, *Journal of the American Society for Information Science*, **51** (6), 543–57.

Foster, A. (2005a) Nonlinear Information Seeking. In Fisher, K. E., Erdelez, S. and McKechnie, L. E. F. (eds), *Theories of Information Behavior*, Information Today, 254–8.

Foster, A. (2005b) A Non-linear Model of Information Seeking Behaviour, *Information Research*, **10** (2), Paper 222, http://informationr.net/ir/10-2/paper222.html.

Foster, A. and Ford, N. (2003) Serendipity and Information Seeking: an empirical study, *Journal of Documentation*, **59** (3), 321–40.

Foster, A. E. (2004) A Nonlinear Model of Information Seeking Behaviour, *Journal of the American Society for Information Science and Technology*, **55** (3), 228–37.

Golub, K. and Lykke, M. (2009) Automated Classification of Web Pages in Hierarchical Browsing, *Journal of Documentation*, **65** (6), 901–25.

Graff, M. (2005) Individual Differences in Hypertext Browsing Strategies, *Behaviour and Information Technology*, **24** (2), 93–9.

Heinström, J. (2005) Fast Surfing, Broad Scanning and Deep Diving: the influence of personality and study approach on students' information-seeking behaviour, *Journal of Documentation*, **61** (2), 228–47.

Heinström, J. (2006) Psychological Factors behind Incidental Information Acquisition,

Library and Information Science Research, **28** (4), 579–94.

Heinström, J. (2010) *From Fear to Flow: personality and information interaction,* Chandos.

Herner, S. (1970) Browsing. In Kent, A., H., Lancour and Nasri, W. Z. (eds), *Encyclopedia of Library and Information Science,* Vol. 3, Marcel Dekker, 408–15.

Hoare, C. and Sorensen, H. (2005) Information Foraging with a Proximity-based Browsing Tool, *Artificial Intelligence Review,* **24** (3–4), 233–52.

Hoeflich, M. H. (2007) Serendipity in the Stacks, Fortuity in the Archives, *Law Library Journal,* **99** (4), 813–27.

Honey, P. and Mumford, A. (1986) *The Manual of Learning Styles,* 2nd edn, Peter Honey.

Jacoby, J. (2005) Optimal Foraging. In Fisher, K. E., Erdelez, S. and McKechnie, L. E. F. (eds), Theories of Information Behaviour, *Information Today,* 259–64.

Jacso, P. (2005) Browsing Indexes of Cited References, *Online Information Review,* **2991,** 107–12.

Jones, R. F. (1971) Noise Level. In Crispin, E. (ed.), *Best SF Five,* Faber.

Kirk. T. (2010) What Has Happened to Browsing Collections in Academic Libraries?, *Library Issues: Briefings for Faculty and Administrators,* **30** (5), May 2010.

Koch, T., Golub, K. and Ardo, A. (2006) Users' Browsing Behaviour in a DDC-based Web Service: a log analysis, *Cataloguing and Classification Quarterly,* **42** (3/4), 163–86.

Kostoff, R. N. et al. (2009) Literature-based Discovery, *Annual Review of Information Science and Technology,* **43,** 241–85.

Kowalski, G. (1997) *Information Retrieval Systems: theory and implementation,* Kluwer Academic.

Makri, S. and Warwick, C. (2010) Information for Inspiration: understanding architects' information seeking and use behaviors to inform design, *Journal of the American Society for Information Science and Technology,* **61** (9), 1745–70.

Marchionini, G. (1995) *Information Seeking in Electronic Environments,* Cambridge University Press.

McBirnie, A. (2008) Seeking Serendipity: the paradox of control, *Aslib Proceedings,* **60** (6), 600–18.

McKenzie, P. J. (2003) A Model of Information Practices in Accounts of Everyday Life Information Seeking, *Journal of Documentation,* **59** (1), 19–40.

Merton, R. K. and Barber, E. (2004) *The Travels and Adventures of Serendipity,* Princeton University Press.

Mobrand, K. A. and Spyridakis, J. H. (2007) Explicitness of Local Navigational Links: comprehension, perceptions of use and browsing behaviour, *Journal of Information Science,* **3391,** 41–61.

Nicholas, D. et al. (2004) Reappraising Information Seeking Behaviour in a Digital Environment: bouncers, checkers, returners, and the like, *Journal of Documentation,* **60** (1), 24–43.

Nutefall, J. E. and Ryder, P. M. (2010) The Serendipitous Research Process, *Journal of*

Academic Librarianship, **3693**, 228–34.

Pálsdóttir, A. (2010) The Connection between Purposive Information Seeking and Information Encountering: a study of Icelanders' health and lifestyle information seeking, *Journal of Documentation*, **66** (2), 224–44.

Perugini, S. (2010) Supporting Multiple Paths to Objects in Information Hierarchies: faceted classification, faceted search and symbolic links, *Information Processing and Management*, **46** (1), 22–43.

Peters, I. (2009) *Folksonomies, Indexing and Retrieval in Web 2.0*, de Gruyter.

Petric, I., Urbancic, T., Cestnik, B. and Macedoni-Luksic, M. (2009) Literature Mining Method: RaJaLink for uncovering relations between biomedical concepts, *Journal of Biomedical Informatics*, **42** (2), 219–27.

Pirolli, P. (2007) *Information Foraging Theory: adaptive interaction with information*, Oxford University Press.

Pirolli, P. and Card, S. K. (1999) Information Foraging, *Psychological Review*, **106** (4), 643–75.

Rice, R. E., McCreadie, M. M. and Chang, S. L. (2001) *Accessing and Browsing Information and Communication*, MIT Press.

Riding, R. and Rayner, S. G. (1998) *Cognitive Styles and Learning Strategies*, David Fulton.

Roe, B. J. (1985) On Line but Out of Mind, *Guardian*, 22 July, readers' letters.

Ross, C. S. (1999) Finding without Seeking: the information encounter in the context of reading for pleasure, *Information Processing and Management*, **35** (6), 783–99.

Ruthven, I. (2008) Interactive Information Retrieval, *Annual Review of Information Science and Technology*, **42**, 43–91.

Schneiderman, B. (2001) *Leonardo's Laptop: human needs and the new computing technologies*, MIT Press.

Shiri, A. (2009) An Examination of Social Tagging Interface Features and Functionalities: an analytical comparison, *Online Information Review*, **33** (5), 901–19.

Spink, A. and Greisdorf, H. (1997) Users' Partial Relevance Judgements during Online Searching, *Online and CD-ROM Review*, **21** (5), 271–80.

Spiteri, L. F. (2010) Incorporating Facets into Social Tagging: an analysis of current trends, *Cataloguing and Classification Quarterly*, **48** (1), 94–109.

Swanson, D. (1990) Medical Literature as a Potential Source of New Knowledge, *Bulletin of the Medical Library Association*, **78** (10), 29–37.

Swanson, D. R. and Smalheiser, N. R. (1999) Implicit Text Linkages between Medline Records: using Arrowsmith as an aid to scientific discovery, *Library Trends*, **4891**, 48–59.

Swanson, D. R., Smalheiser, N. R. and Torvik, V. I. (2006) Ranking Indirect Connections in Literature-based Discovery: the role of medical subject headings, *Journal of the American Society for Information Science and Technology*, **57** (11), 1427–39.

Tang, M. (2007) Browsing and Searching in a Faceted Information Space: a naturalistic study of PubMed users' interaction with a display tool, *Journal of the American*

Society for Information Science and Technology, **58** (13), 1998–2006.

Toms, E. G. (2002) Information Interaction: providing a framework for information architecture, *Journal of the American Society for Information Science and Technology*, **5391**, 855–62.

Urquhart, D. J. (1976) National Lending/Reference Libraries or Libraries of First Resort, *BLL Review*, **4** (1), 7–10.

Vickery, J.E. (1977), A Note in Defence of Browsing, *BLL Review*, **5** (3), 110.

Wade, S. J., Willett, P. and Bawden, D. (1989) SIBRIS: the Sandwich Interactive Browsing and Ranking Information System, *Journal of Information Science*, **15** (4/5), 249–60.

Weeber, M. et al. (2001) Using Concepts in Literature-based Discovery: simulating Swanson's Raynaud-fish oil and migraine-magnesium discoveries, *Journal of the American Society for Information Science and Technology*, **52** (7), 548–57.

Westerman, S. J., Collins, J. and Cribbin, T. (2005) Browsing a Document Collection Represented in Two- and Three-dimensional Virtual Information Space, *International Journal of Human-Computer Studies*, **62** (6), 713–36.

Westman, S. (2009) Image Users' Needs and Searching Behaviour. In Göker, A. and Davies, J. (eds), *Information Retrieval: searching in the 21st century*, Wiley, 63–83.

Wiggins, J. S. (ed.) (1996) *The Five-factor Model of Personality: theoretical perspectives*, Guilford Press.

Willett, P. (2000) Textual and Chemical Information Processing: different domains but similar algorithms, *Information Research*, **5** (2), Paper 69, http://InformationR.net/ir/5-2/paper69.html.

Willett, P. (2008) From Chemical Documentation to Chemoinformatics: 50 years of chemical information science, *Journal of Information Science*, **34** (4), 477–99.

Willett, P. (2009) Similarity Methods in Chemoinformatics, *Annual Review of Information Science and Technology*, **43**, 3–71.

Williamson, K. (1998) Discovered by Chance: the role of incidental information acquisition in an ecological model of information use, *Library and Information Science Research*, **20** (1), 23–40.

Wilson, T. D. (1999) Models in Information Behaviour Research, *Journal of Documentation*, **37** (1), 3–15.

Wilson, T. D. (2005) Evolution in Information Behavior Modelling: Wilson's model, in Fisher, K. E., Erdelez, S. and McKechnie, L. E. F. (eds), *Theories of Information Behavior*, Information Today, 31–6.

Yuan, X. and Belkin, N. J. (2010) Investigating Information Retrieval Support Techniques for Different Information-seeking Strategies, *Journal of the American Society for Information Science and Technology*, **61** (8), 1543–63.

2

Classification revisited: a web of knowledge

Aida Slavic

Introduction

The vision of the semantic web is gradually unfolding and taking shape through a web of linked data, a part of which is built by capturing semantics stored in existing knowledge organization systems (KOS), subject metadata and resource metadata. The content of vast bibliographic collections is currently categorized by some widely used bibliographic classification and we may soon see them being mined for information and linked in a meaningful way across the web. Bibliographic classifications are designed for knowledge mediation, which offers both a rich terminology and different ways in which concepts can be categorized and related to each other in the universe of knowledge. From 1990 to 2010 they have been used in various resource discovery services on the web, and they continue to be used to support information integration in a number of international digital library projects. In this chapter we will revisit some of the ways in which universal classifications, as language-independent concept schemes, can assist humans and computers in structuring and presenting information and formulating queries. Most importantly, we will highlight issues important to understanding bibliographic classifications, identifying both their unused potential and their technical limitations.

Background

Classifications are created using the intellectual power of ontological observation and analysis and reflect whichever approach one decides to take in defining and grouping things. Whatever the motive for their creation, classifications are logically and semantically organized schemes of concepts representing some kind of reality and, as such, are essential and versatile tools for the representation and visualization of a knowledge space. A classification, by nature, cannot serve all purposes; however, if it is universal with respect to knowledge coverage and structured in a comprehensive, detailed, highly elaborate and logical way, it is likely to be more versatile than a scheme created for one single subject, system or task.

Bibliographic or documentary classifications are a special kind of knowledge classification designed for the mediation of knowledge. Their unique feature is that they are not concerned with objects or entities, as other knowledge classifications, but rather with subjects, i.e. the ways in which entities are described in documents. Bibliographic classifications will systematize phenomena and the topics that can be studied in relation to these phenomena, but will also provide the vocabulary necessary to denote types of knowledge presentation, points of view, the targeted audience or form of document. As subject is a complex construct, which ought to be described with a series of concepts in various relationships, classification can also provide rules on how to express complex interactions between phenomena of knowledge as they appear in documents. The oldest and the best-known type of bibliographic classification are library classifications, which are created primarily for the physical arrangement of library shelves. The fact that a classification is created for shelf arrangement, and not for detailed indexing for the purposes of metadata-based information retrieval, may influence its structure and its vocabulary, as will be explained in the following sections. But, whatever their original purpose, general bibliographic classifications are known to be complex systems.

Although there are many classifications, the three most internationally used general bibliographic classifications are Dewey Decimal Classification (DDC), Universal Decimal Classification (UDC) and Library of Congress Classification (LCC). They are used in the greatest number of countries and bibliographic collections and are considered *de facto* standards in information exchange. The main reason that these classifications prevail is a complex set of circumstances primarily related to the power of their ownership, services based on them and their continuous maintenance and development. DDC, although originally created for the shelf arrangement of a single college library, started to be widely used in Anglo-American libraries from the 19th century onwards, as the best classification for shelf arrangement at the time. Its use throughout and beyond the 20th century was promoted by the Online Computer Library Center (OCLC) bibliographic service. UDC, originally created as an indexing language for an international universal bibliography project in 1895, gained widespread use through the international presence of its previous owner, the International Federation of Information (FID), which supported its development, translation into more than 30 languages and its world-wide distribution. LCC's popularity can be attributed to its governmentally controlled and well-supported administration, the speed with which works are classified and the availability of LCC classmarks on Library of Congress catalogue cards, rather than to its inherent structural quality (Marcella and Newton, 1994, 60). Circumstances in the bibliographic domain are such that Colon Classification (CC), which is certainly the most theoretically praised library classification, is barely used, while Bliss Bibliographic Classification (BC2), which is supposed to demonstrate an excellence in classification design, is only 60% complete and is also barely used. There are also a number of national general classification systems, but their use is confined to a single country or language, which limits their role in the context of global information integration.

Intellectual indexing and classification requires a high level of expertise and is an expensive and time-consuming process, which may not be suited to, or required for, all information-retrieval scenarios. For most text-retrieval tasks, various models of automatic text processing and advanced techniques such as statistical models, language models or machine learning will perform well. However, not all documents are available in digital form and not all digital documents are textual, in the same language or in the same script. Equally, not all digital collections are available or accessible in an open networked environment and not all will lend themselves easily to processing by otherwise successful data- and knowledge-mining methods. The task of merging and integrating information contained in legacy collections into what may be a web of knowledge is still ahead of us.

National bibliographies of most countries continuously collect, describe and classify everything that is published in their respective country, by their citizens or in their official languages. This practice has existed for over a century, in some instances even longer, and has led to the creation of large bibliographic collections, only parts of which may be available in digital form. Although this may hardly be comparable with the scale of information available on the web, we are still talking about hundreds and hundreds of millions of documents published in numerous languages all around the world from the beginning of literacy to date. We can assume that in the foreseeable future libraries will continue to classify books for the purpose of collection management, and we know that legacy bibliographic data is something we will try to preserve.

The fact that document collections world-wide are classified using bibliographic classification systems may play a significant role in enabling subject searching across these collections. A significant increase in the use of classification in various information-integration and discovery services from 1990 to 2010 clearly indicated such a trend. In the following section we will highlight some shared structural features of bibliographic classifications that are of particular importance for their use in information retrieval and discovery.

Classification, how does it work?

In Figure 2.1 we see two ways of representing a knowledge field for the purpose of knowledge browsing: one system using natural-language terms and the other employing a systematic or classificatory arrangement.

Antineutrinos	539.1	Nuclear physics. Atomic physics. Molecular physics
Antineutrons	539.12	Elementary and simple particles
Antiprotons	539.123/.124	Leptons. Including: Muons
Atomic physics	539.123	Neutrinos
Baryons	539.123.6	Antineutrinos
Beta-particles	539.124	Electrons (including beta-particles)
Bosons	539.124.6	Positrons
Electrons	539.125/.126	Hadrons. Baryons and mesons
Hadrons	539.125	Nucleons
Hyperons	539.125.4	Protons
Leptons	539.125.46	Antiprotons
Mesons	539.125.5	Neutrons
Mesons	539.125.56	Antineutrons
Molecular physics	539.126.3	Mesons
Muons	539.126.4	Resonances
Neutrinos	539.126.6	Hyperons
Neutrons		
Nuclear physics		
Nuclei		
Nucleons		
Positrons		
Protons		
Resonances		

Figure 2.1 *Presenting knowledge for browsing*

If we use words for indexing, the only way we can mechanically display the subject index of a collection is alphabetically. Two concepts will find themselves in close proximity not because of their semantic similarity, but rather owing to the accidence of their names. Classification, on the other hand, groups concepts semantically, according to the closeness of their meaning. But in order to 'fix' this systematic organization, classification needs a notational device: a numeric, alphabetic or alphanumeric symbol that represents the class arrangement and supports its mechanical manipulation. Notation is the shortest possible way of expressing sometimes very complex subjects and is very useful in labelling physical documents or metadata for the purpose of systematic arrangement. In Figure 2.1 we see an example of a numerical, decimal (fractional) notation, where each digit represents a decimal level that corresponds to the level of subdivision and in which the dot after every third digit is inserted only for the convenience of reading. We call this type of notation hierarchically expressive: the longer the notation, the more specific the class it represents, and by removing the last digit we automatically broaden the class. Not all notations are decimal or hierarchically expressive; they can be a simple ordering device, as is the case with LCC and BC2 (Figure 2.2)

Q	Science
QD1-999	Chemistry
QD241-441	Organic chemistry

Example from LCC

AZ	Science
C	Chemistry
CO	Organic

Examples from BC 2

Figure 2.2 *Notation used as an ordering device*

Notations (classmarks) represent the class meaning in a universal way, no matter how many terms we use to describe it or in which language these terms may be. For example, if we use 536 to represent Heat (Thermodynamics) in the bibliographic services of China, Russia or the UK we will be able to search for documents on this topic irrespective of the language or script in which they are published (Figure 2.3)

DDC		**UDC**		
536	Heat	536	Heat. Thermodynamics	[English]
	Chaleur		Chaleur. Thermodynamique	[French]
	Теплота		Тепло . Термодинамика	[Russian]
	热、热力学、		热	[Chinese]

Examples from UDC and DDC summaries

Figure 2.3 *Notation used to represent meaning*

Precisely because classification uses notation for indexing, which is practical for human communication, word access to schedules is of extreme importance. Notation descriptions, technically called captions, are one source of language terms, but they are to a large extent only indicative and are designed for the purpose of schedule presentation. Therefore, all widely used classification systems have carefully constructed and detailed subject-alphabetical indexes. In addition to this, databases for the management of classification will usually be designed to generate a caption hierarchy and/or chain indexes (contextualized terms within the hierarchy). Many online systems provide controlled keywords attached to each class as well as mappings to subject-heading systems if appropriate. The importance of word access to classification codes is such that alphabetical indexes to classification have become sophisticated terminology tools in their own right. For instance, DDC's Relative Index, which relates concepts and terms scattered across the scheme, is widely accepted as one of the finest examples. UDC editions in different languages are known to be published with various kinds of indexes, from a relative chain index to indexes in the form of a thesaurus. S. R. Ranganathan, the author of CC, particularly favoured an alphabetical index in the form of a chain index.

The role of logical and perspective hierarchies

The most prominent characteristic of all classifications is hierarchy: the organization of concepts into a sequence of classes based on various principles of division, following the order of classes from broader to narrower. Hierarchy is important because it determines the meaning of a concept, which operates above the level of language. For example, the relationship between the concept of *carrot* and the concept of *root vegetable* is always the same and universally understood, irrespective of which words in which language we use to name these entities. However, when classifications present an entire universe of knowledge they need to deploy several different structural and organizational mechanisms, logical hierarchy being only one of them.

Logical hierarchy

The general principle of a valid hierarchy is that all members of a class share at least one characteristic. Each class contains a number of subclasses and all members of a subclass are contained in the class above and inherit its characteristics. These are the principles of a logical hierarchy that may be built on three kinds of hierarchical relationships: generic or proper hierarchic relationships (genera–species, where each member is a *kind of* the class above); partitive relationships (whole–part, where each member is part of the class above); class–member and instance relationships (each member is an instantiation of a class or simply its member based on an arbitrary characteristic). The most typical characteristic of a logical hierarchy is the fact that each entity will have only one place in the hierarchy. Every entity will have one broader class, the property of subdivision will be transitive and the logic of the hierarchy will support broadening, narrowing or exploding searches in the process of information retrieval.

For instance, a logical hierarchy of languages can help to avoid confusion between the term *Tepehua*, one of the Totonacan languages, and *Tepehuan*, a Uto-Aztecan language. While it is easy to confuse the names (Tepehua/Tepehuan), the hierarchy and its notational representation indicate that these are two entirely different concepts (Figure 2.4).

Hierarchy is even more important in cases of polysemy, when the meaning of a word can become evident only through its contextualization within a

= 82	Indigenous languages of western North American Coast, Mexico and Yucatan
...	
=821	Penutian, Huave, Utian, Totonacan, Mixe-Zoque languages
=821.22	Totonacan languages
=821.221	**Tepehua**
...	
=822	Uto-Aztecan and Kiowa-Tanoan languages
=822.2	Uto-Aztecan languages
=822.24	Southern Uto-Aztecan languages
=822.248	**Tepehuan**

Example from UDC MRF (2010)

Figure 2.4 *Differentiation of concepts in a notational representation of hierarchy*

hierarchy. For instance, the meaning of a polyseme such as cell will depend on whether it is placed within the broader class of cytology, or subsumed to the concept of prison or to the concept of electrochemical equipment. The need for disambiguation increases with the size of the knowledge area covered and becomes very important in searching large collections comprising numerous forms of knowledge.

Perspective or aspect hierarchies

General bibliographic classifications arrange the universe of knowledge by placing different forms of knowledge into main classes (macro level) according to some existing, widely accepted theories of knowledge organization. This is determined by the basic function of knowledge mediation, which is facilitating access to knowledge and its use: phenomena and topics that are studied and sought together are placed together. By respecting this principle, topics for, e.g. sport fishermen, such as kinds of fishing, fishing by different methods and tools, fishing by type of fish, by place, by time, etc., will be collocated together. As soon as we start organizing knowledge in this way we will find that many phenomena will be of interest to many fields of knowledge: gold will be studied as a chemical element in chemistry, as a product in the mining industry or as a material in arts and crafts. This kind of approach to knowledge organization, in which phenomena are subsumed to the form of knowledge within which they are studied, is known as a disciplinary knowledge organization.

Concepts organized in main classes corresponding to disciplines and subdisciplines will therefore be related not only through a logical hierarchy (subordination and superordination) but may find themselves in collateral relationships, since the same concepts will appear in numerous other hierarchies within the scheme (Bhattacharyya, 1979). This will result in perspective or aspect hierarchies (Svenonius, 1997). Figure 2.5 shows the occurrence of the concept of shark in different knowledge fields.

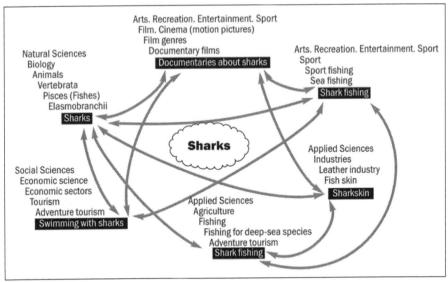

Figure 2.5 *'Distributed relatives', one concept in different fields of knowledge*

A single logical hierarchy will support broadening, narrowing or exploding searches within the same subdivision. Perspective hierarchies are a unique feature of universal bibliographic classifications that have an important impact on information retrieval because they can support concept association, contextualization and disambiguation across different fields of knowledge. The fact that the same concept can appear in different hierarchies leads to four important structural features typical of bibliographic classifications:

1   **Syndetic structure**, based on the large number of associative relationships ('see also' references) that are established between classes across the entire scheme (Figure 2.6).

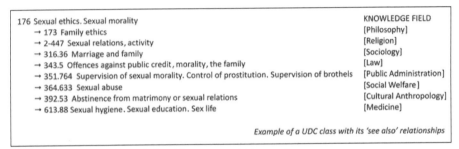

Figure 2.6 *Associative relationships in a syndetic structure*

Not all bibliographic classifications have the same affinity towards connecting distributed relatives. This is usually a feature of classifications that are created to function as a coherent system (e.g. DDC, UDC). LCC and BC2 are developed as series of special classifications, and associative relationships between different fields of knowledge are significantly less frequent, and in many cases non-existent.

2   **Relative subject alphabetical index**, constituting a standard part of a classification system and serving to connect 'distributed relatives' and support retrieval and contextualization of search, as in Figure 2.7.

3   **Separation of common concepts** (isolates) from classification of knowledge. Owing to their frequency, general concepts are organized as separate facet hierarchies or tables, usually called common auxiliaries, so that they can be reused and combined with

Marriage	306.81
arts	700.454.3
customs	392.5
ethics	173
religion	205.63
...	
folklore	398.27
law	346.016

Example of Relative Index (DDC)

Figure 2.7 *Relative index connecting 'distributed relatives'*

concepts in knowledge fields. This approach can be seen in DDC, UDC, CC, BC2 and many other general knowledge schemes (Figure 2.8).

4   **Parallel divisions**, a typical feature of many bibliographic classifications, and occurring frequently between disciplines that deal with the same phenomena: Natural Sciences and Applied Sciences; Languages, Linguistics and Literatures; Geography and History etc. For instance, the

Place facet		Combinations with Place	
(4)	Europe	027	General libraries
(46)	Countries of the Iberian Peninsula	027(469)	General libraries in Portugal
(469)	Portugal		
		338.48	Tourism
		338.48(469)	Tourism in Portugal
		726	Church buildings
		726(469)	Church buildings in Portugal
		91	Regional geography
		91(469)	Regional geography of Portugal
		94	History
		94(469)	History of Portugal

Example of common concepts in use (UDC)

Figure 2.8 *Combination of a common concept and concepts in knowledge fields*

classification of plants in Botany or animals in Zoology will be used to build hierarchies in Palaeobotany or in Agriculture. In the example from DDC in Figure 2.9 we can see how a concept hierarchy of Insects from class 590 Animals is not replicated in class 560 Paleozoology. Instead, there is an instruction explaining that fossils of insects should be built using numbers from the class hierarchy at 590 when required.

560	Paleontology. Paleozoology	590	Animals
565	Fossil Arthropoda	595	Arthropoda
565.7	**Insecta**	**595.7**	**Insecta**
	Add to base number 565.7	595.72	Apterygota
	the number following 595.72-595.79	595.73	Exopterygota (Hemimetabola)
	e.g. Coleoptera 565.76	595.74	Mecoptera, Trichoptera, Neuroptera...
566	Fossil Chordata	...	
...		595.79	Hymenoptera

Example from DDC (22)

Figure 2.9 *Example of parallel division*

Analytico-synthetic principle in building classifications

The number of knowledge forms that are selected as a macro structure of knowledge (main classes) and the logic of their sequence in bibliographic classifications is usually based on some widely accepted philosophical knowledge classifications, which are themselves subject to many theoretical discussions and criticism. It is well known that any such disciplinary classification is inevitably rigid with respect to the dynamic nature of knowledge and biased in terms of a cultural or philosophical point of view. No matter how frequently we change this view, it will always be a single, frozen snapshot of a world at a given time.

To address this problem, bibliographic classifications have developed various mechanisms, methods and techniques that operate at the micro level of a classification and help in resolving intra-, inter- and cross-disciplinary relationships as they appear in the subject of documents. This is resolved in three ways:

- Identification of isolates or general concepts that are frequently reused across knowledge and their placement in separate facets. These would usually be isolates of place, time, languages, forms of documents, general characteristics of various kinds (as explained in the previous section).
- Organization of concepts within a knowledge field into a set of mutually exclusive broad-concept categories that can be combined to express the composite nature of any given subject and all aspects from which a phenomenon may be studied and viewed within a single field of knowledge.

- Syntactical rules and devices to express relations between concepts from different disciplines.

Classification schemes created in such a way are called analytico-synthetic.

Facet analytical theory

If we take a document such as 'Economic development in Europe after 1945', we recognize some general categories of elements: 'economy' is the main subject, 'development' is a process, 'Europe' is a place, and 'after 1945' is a time. These categorizations are valid whether we analyse the content of the document or are trying to formulate our query when searching. It has been widely accepted in the theory of content analysis and indexing that subject topicality can be analysed and expressed with a high level of accuracy if we follow a particular set of fundamental concept categories (Hutchins, 1975; Langridge, 1989; Broughton, 2004).

Although a kind of categorical analysis was intuitively built into the UDC back in the early 1900s as a way of structuring schedules, the categorical structural principle was not properly analysed and introduced into classification theory before the work of the Indian classificationist S. R. Ranganathan in the 1930s. He proposed five fundamental categories of concepts or fundamental facet categories: personality, matter, energy, space and time, as a categorical framework for building classification for all fields of knowledge, and proved his theory by building his Colon Classification (CC), the first fully faceted bibliographic classification system. The principle of facet analysis in organization of knowledge was widely discussed and was adopted as an efficient technique in subject organization from the 1960s onward, under the name of *facet analytical theory*. The extended set of 13 fundamental facet categories (Thing–Kind–Part–Property–Material–Process–Operation–Patient–Product–Byproduct–Agent–Place–Time) was proposed by the Classification Research Group (CRG), the British group of classification experts, in the 1960s (Hutchins, 1975). Taking this as a fundamental principle, the CRG commenced its work of restructuring Bliss Bibliographic Classification into a new BC2 faceted scheme in the 1970s. The principle has been tested ever since and used in building thesauri and classifications.

Facet analytical theory as proposed and implemented in BC2 not only defines the principles for the analysis of a subject field and its categorical structuring in a bottom-up fashion but suggests what is defined as the correct order of the facets in the schedule (filial order) as well as the strict order of citing categorical elements in a complex subject statement (citation order). Once concepts are hierarchically organized into their respective broader facet categories, their arrangement and combination is fixed and mechanized through an inexpressive notational system (Figure 2.10) (Broughton, 2004).

PBK	Sacred books
...	
PIJ	Vedic religion
PIJ BK	Sacred books
PIJ C	Samhitas
PIJ D	Trayi Vidya

Example of notation from BC 2

Figure 2.10 *Arrangement of concepts in facet categories*

In the example in Figure 2.10 the notation itself does not indicate that class PIJ C Samhitas is superordinated to class PIJ D Trayi Vidhya or that the notation of class PIJ BK Sacred books is composed of PBK Sacred books and PIJ Vedic religion. The notation in BC2 has primarily 'ordinal' value because the use of the classification is assumed to serve the purpose of shelf arrangement, for which the brevity of notation is most important. Faceted classifications can also have a hierarchically and syntactically expressive notation (Broughton and Slavic, 2007), as shown in Figure 2.11.

[By Language]		[By Literary form]		[By Period]		[By Document form]	
A	English literature	-1	poetry	aa	old period	01	polygraphic work
B	Hindi Literature	-2	drama	ab	middle period	02	collected works
C	Arabic Literature	-3	prose	ac	modern period	03	selected works
...			...		...	031	anthologies
						...	

A-1aa031	English literature - poetry - old period - anthologies
B-2ac02	Hindi literature - drama - modern period - collected works
C-1ac03	Arabic literature - poetry - modern period - selected works
C-3ac031	Arabic literature - prose - modern period - anthologies

Model of syntactically expressive notation

Figure 2.11 *Syntactically expressive notation in faceted classification*

The first and most important step in building a classification structure of this kind is deciding what constitutes the main thing or entity facet for that particular knowledge field. Once this is decided, the other broad facet categories are formed around the main facet. A decision of what is the main facet in, for example, Information Science (services/institutions or operations/functions or documents), or Medicine (organs, physiology, diseases, patients or treatments) is an arbitrary decision by classification designers and is based on their perception of what may be the most logical or most useful order of subject within a field of knowledge, for an assumed application.

The difference in the number of fundamental categories between CC and BC2 clearly indicates that there are some issues concerning the very 'fundamental' nature of these categories (Hjørland, 2006). The universality of the principle can also be questioned with respect to the fact that CRG facet categories work well in natural and applied sciences but are not as easy to apply in social sciences and humanities (Svenonius, 1997). In addition, the explanation of this principle in building a classification 'bottom up', based on literary warrant, seems to have little practical merit, since, in reality, the terminology for building a classification has to be aligned with user warrant, leading to an actual alignment of two different views: those of users and those of experts (Giess, Wild and McMahon, 2008).

Other approaches: facet analysis and free-faceted classification

Even though this does not entirely agree with the facet analytical theory, organizing concepts into mutually exclusive facets is viewed as a flexible approach whenever one wants to manipulate, co-ordinate and reorder facet hierarchies to achieve different arrangements and emphasis. Such is the idea of 'freely faceted classification' as proposed by Gnoli and Mei (2006). Based on this is the proposal for free facets to be combined with a classification of phenomena, in contrast to disciplinary classifications. In such a scheme knowledge phenomena are not subsumed to disciplines, but vice versa, following the tradition of Subject Classification by J. Brown, which was a classification of phenomena used at the beginning of the 20th century in a number of American and British libraries (Szostak and Gnoli, 2008)

Although it has little to do with the principles of facet analytical theory, the advantage of organizing entities, objects or concepts into facets to improve hierarchy management, display and browsing has also become apparent to web designers. This kind of vocabulary organization is widely accepted as good practice outside the specific field of subject analysis and knowledge classification and is popularized in the browsing interfaces of portals, commercial websites and content management systems (La Barre, 2006; Vickery, 2008).

Relating subjects from different fields of knowledge or phase relationships

One of the most prominent issues in subject indexing arises from the fact that documents may represent and relate subjects from different fields of knowledge: 'The use of granite in altar-domes in mediaeval churches of Italy', 'Scholarly production in bibliographies of European national libraries', 'Application of computers in education', 'Bibliography of rare books'. Synthesis based on facet analytical theory, as described in the previous section, helps to resolve the situation in subject indexing when we can assume a single principal concept modified by a cluster of subsidiary concepts, which can be analysed and presented as a compound notational expression. Classifications designed for the arrangement of library shelves will assume that, no matter how many subjects are discussed in a document, it will always be classified in place, depending on which subject is deemed to be more appropriate for given content.

Classifications designed for detailed indexing and retrieval usually have a set of notational symbols (relators) for establishing relationships between two or more independent or otherwise unrelated subjects. For instance, UDC uses + symbols when subjects are connected and studied as juxtaposed, e.g. 73+75 Sculpture and Painting; a colon when subjects are studied in a simple relation, e.g. 73:75 Relationship between Sculpture and Painting. These kinds of relationship are termed *phase relationships* and they have been thoroughly studied and widely discussed in the theory of classification and indexing. Jean Perreault offered a detailed schema of these relators based on the earlier work by J. E. L. Farradane, J. C. Gardin and E. Grolier (Hutchins, 1975).

Enumerative vs analytico-synthetic classifications

Traditionally, classification theory makes a distinction between enumerative and analytico-synthetic classification schemes, and this frequently causes confusion because many classifications combine these principles in different ways. Both approaches to structuring schedules have their advantages and their shortcomings when it comes to their application in information retrieval or information integration in an online environment.

Analytico-synthetic classifications allow the synthesis of concepts in the process of indexing and their coordination in the process of searching, i.e. parsing of composite subject expressions to their composite elements. This means that although subjects such as 'history of mathematics', 'wars in Africa in the 19th century', 'English poetry' or 'herbal medicine in melanoma therapy' do not appear in the schedules enumerated as such, they can be expressed. The obvious advantage of this approach is that such schedules are suited to covering subjects in an unlimited way, in great detail, with a smaller but logically structured vocabulary. The disadvantage is that when one scans these schedules in order to extract the vocabulary, the analysis produces only a very partial picture of the actual subject coverage. To address this issue, analytico-synthetic classifications try to enumerate combinations (BC2) and others try to go half way by listing a selection of examples of combination (UDC).

Enumerative classifications are typically created for the arrangement of library shelves and their main concern is short classification codes (for both simple and complex subjects) that are easy to file and that take little space on book spines. The easiest way to achieve this is to publish a scheme with a selection of the subject combinations that are most likely to appear in an imaginary collection and assign to them simple, short, ordering notations. The disadvantages are twofold: limited power in indexing, as obviously one cannot plan for all combinations of subjects, and occasional compressions of subdivisions into a single class, resulting in illogical and awkward placement of compound subjects.

The example in Figure 2.12 shows how DDC enumerates the subdivision Organizations by place. Each of these composite classes is assigned a simple notation. In UDC, when determination of place is required the code of place is taken from the place facet, i.e. common auxiliaries of place, and combined with the main subject notation.

Enumerative classification (DDC)		Analytico-synthetic classification (UDC)		
060	General organizations & museum science	06	Organizations of a general nature	
061	Organizations in North America		*Examples of combination:*	
062	Organizations in British Isles; in England		06(7)	Organizations - North America
063	Organizations in central Europe; in Germany		06(41)	Organizations - British Isles
064	Organizations in France & Monaco		06(430)	Organizations - Germany
...			...	
070	News media, journalism & publishing	070	Newspapers. The Press. Journalism	
071	Newspapers in North America		*Examples of combination:*	
072	Newspapers in British Isles; in England		070(7)	Newspapers - North America
073	Newspapers in central Europe; in Germany		070(41)	Newspapers - British Isles
074	Newspapers in France & Monaco		070(430)	Newspapers - Germany
...			...	

Example from DDC and UDC Summaries

Figure 2.12 *Comparison of enumerative and analytico-synthetic classification*

From the example in Figure 2.12 it is clear why enumerative classifications require larger schedules to achieve the same indexing specificity, hence LCC has over 200,000 and significantly weaker indexing power than UDC, which has only 68,000 classes. Care should be taken not to generalize and assume that 'enumerative' classifications such as DDC or LCC could not use synthesis and allow the building of numbers to a certain extent. Equally, analytico-synthetic classifications can include pre-built notations in their schedules.

Classification in information retrieval

From what has been said so far about logical and aspect hierarchies and alphabetical indexes attached to classification, we would expect that any information system holding classification data supports the following two simple term-search scenarios: a) a systematic display of results allowing for semantic search expansion as shown in the left illustration in Figure 2.13; b) a systematic display of results enabling disambiguation and contextualization of search terms within perspective hierarchies, as in the right illustration.

The most obvious place to look for good practice in using classification data to support subject searching, as illustrated in Figure 2.13 oveleaf, would be library online public access catalogues (OPACs). Paradoxically, this is not the case and this fact has been puzzling researchers for decades. Studies have so far confirmed very poor use of classification, in spite of obvious advantages in its

hadrons		Search
		Hits
539.12	Elementary Particles	132
539.125/.126	Hadrons. Baryons and mesons	58
539.125	Nucleons	38
539.125.4	Protons	5
539.125.46	Antiprotons	2
539.125.5	Neutrons	7
539.125.56	Antineutrons	1
539.126.3	Mesons	9
539.126.5	Resonances	11
539.126.6	Hyperons	6

rabbit		Search
		Hits
569.32	Zoology: Rodentia and Lagomorpha	7
632.935.7	Protection of Crops	3
636.92	Animal Husbandry: Domestic Rabbits	38
636.92.045	Animal Husbandry: Domestic Rabbits. Pets	10
636.932	Animal Husbandry: Rodents kept for fur	9
639.112	Hunting: Small game generally	22
641.8	Cooking: Main dishes	2
677.534	Textile industry: Hare fur. Rabbit fur	8

Figure 2.13 *Classification supporting simple term search*

use (Wajenberg, 1983; Svenonius, 1983; Cochrane and Markey, 1985; Markey, 1986, 1996; Hildreth, 1991; Hancock, 1987; Markey and Weller, 1996). At the same time surveys of OPACs indicate that users experience problems in finding the correct search term so as to increase recall when results are too few and increase precision when too many items are found (Larson, 1991; Yu and Young, 2004). In spite of the significant advances in database and interface technology, recent research of subject-access functionality conducted on the same library systems in 2003 and 2008 in Italy shows very poor general performance of most of the major vendor systems, and almost no change over a five-year period (Casson, Fabrizzi and Slavic, 2009).

The problems encountered when searching classification in library systems reside in a clear discrepancy between the composite structure and dense classification notation semantics, and their primitive processing in library systems. In the 1980s, Wajenberg (1983) recommended extending MARC codes for DDC so as to use shelfmarks for improving subject searching of bibliographic data. Cochrane and Markey (1985) provided an exhaustive list of classification data elements needed to support searching and browsing of DDC. This effectively represented a subject authority control framework that was independent of the bibliographic description and was capable of serving classification maintenance, distribution and its subsequent use in information retrieval.

Although by the 1990s librarians had fully embraced authority control for managing names, it took some time for the same model of the central management of vocabulary to be proposed as a solution for supporting subject data, including classification. Mandel (1995) emphasized the obvious fact that access points to classification data ought to be controlled centrally, and independently of bibliographic records. Subject authority control significantly changes the way classification is displayed, browsed and searched; it allows independent access to notation, notation hierarchy, associative relationships and word access to classification. Figure 2.14 shows the way subject access points based on classification are managed in three languages in the authority file of the Network of Libraries and Information Centers in Switzerland (NEBIS), www.nebis.ch.

Cross-references - ETH Subjects - HADRONS (PHYSIQUE DES PARTICULES ÉLÉMENTAIRES) : fre : 539.12,000.1

Click on the tag in the left column to jump to this heading in the Browse List.
Click on an underlined heading to create a set of records related to it.
Click on the browser's *back* button to return to your place in the Browse List.

UDC	539.12,000.1
Term	HADRONEN (TEILCHENPHYSIK)
Term	HADRONS (PARTICLE PHYSICS)
Term	HADRONS (PHYSIQUE DES PARTICULES ÉLÉMENTAIRES)
Broader term	ELEMENTARTEILCHENPHYSIK : 539.12
Broader term	PARTICLE PHYSICS : 539.12
Broader term	PHYSIQUE DES PARTICULES ÉLÉMENTAIRES : 539.12
Narrower term	BARYONEN (TEILCHENPHYSIK) : 539.12,000.11
Narrower term	BARYONS (PARTICLE PHYSICS) : 539.12,000.11
Narrower term	BARYONS (PHYSIQUE DES PARTICULES ÉLÉMENTAIRES) : 539.12,000.11
Narrower term	MESONEN (TEILCHENPHYSIK) : 539.126
Narrower term	MESONS (PARTICLE PHYSICS) : 539.126
Narrower term	MÉSONS (PHYSIQUE DES PARTICULES ÉLÉMENTAIRES) : 539.126
Related term	NUKLEONEN (TEILCHENPHYSIK) : 539.125
Related term	NUCLEONS (PARTICLE PHYSICS) : 539.125
Related term	NUCLÉONS (PHYSIQUE DES PARTICULES ÉLÉMENTAIRES) : 539.125
System No	000015327

Figure 2.14 *Subject authority record, OPAC display*

The first breakthrough as regards classification use in library systems was in 1992, when the USMARC Format for Classification Data was created as an independent authority format. The creation of this format was driven by the plans for the conversion of LCC, to which purpose it was effectively used in 1993 (Guenther, 1994). This standard was later superseded by MARC 21 Concise Format for Classification Data, which has since been updated and improved through subsequent versions. Although the format was, theoretically, presented as a general solution, in practice it was based on LCC and DDC structures and is, for this reason, better suited to enumerative classifications. The next opportunity to 'rethink' and improve machine readability was occasioned by work on the UNIMARC authority format for classification data that was meant to be improved to support analytico-synthetic systems. This standard is still awaiting its official completion (Slavic and Cordeiro, 2004; Slavic, 2008).

In parallel to the above-mentioned automation of library systems, the publishers and owners of DDC and UDC created more advanced database tools, primarily to facilitate the maintenance and publishing of classifications. The issue of classification data's being able to support user-friendly hierarchical browsing, semantic linking and facet control became central to classification owners when publishers started selling access to schedules on CD-ROM (from 1995) and on the web (from 2001). The contribution by the publishers of classification data to the automation of classification is significant, for when a classification is converted into a machine-readable format the same data can be used to support various tools for machine-assisted indexing or authority-control tools for supporting information retrieval (Markey, 2006). As more and more classification data are distributed to users as files that can be ingested into information systems, the concern over the inability of bibliographic standards to handle these data is becoming greater. Fortunately, the development of formats and standards for sharing not only classification but all other KOSs has exceeded the limits of specific domains and has been an active area of W3C development over the past ten years.

Bibliographic classifications on the web 1990–2010
Subject gateways, hubs and portals
The idea that bibliographic classification can be used to 'organize the web' was very appealing to web developers at the beginning of the 1990s, when the internet was predominantly academic, cultural and research-orientated. This reflected a strong commitment to interoperability and standardization in information sharing. Web development in the mid-1990s was marked by numerous research projects for building quality subject gateways (SGs). This trend was especially strong in the UK, where a number of SGs were developed within the Electronic Libraries Programme (eLib). In 1999 some of these services joined the Resource Discovery Network (RDN) consisting of subject hubs such as SOSIG (social sciences hub), EMC (engineering, maths, computing hub) and Humbul (humanities hub). This led to a further federation of services that shared the same harvesting, metadata population and indexing tools and eventually evolved into a hub called Intute (www.intute.ac.uk) in 2006, a catalogue of quality, selected internet resources built from the records of eight subject services (Kerr, 2009).

In the beginning, the main characteristic of these quality SGs was that they all used UDC and DDC outlines as the basic browsing structure. As services expanded to include more subjects and more subject-specific indexing languages, and as the number of resources requiring description expanded with the growth of the web, so SGs ceased to use UDC or DDC for the subject browsing interface. This was a logical consequence of the fact that services needed to provide browsing shortcuts to subject areas, some of which were on the fifth or sixth levels of general classification subdivision and, as such, generated an unnecessarily long sequence of browsing steps. Classification was, however, retained for content indexing by the system 'behind the scenes' so as to support consistency in indexing independently of the browsing function (Slavic, 2006).

Automatic classification of web resources

An important aspect of the use of classification in SGs was that it led to an exploration of automatic classification of textual web resources using bibliographic classifications. GERHARD – German Harvest Automated Retrieval and Directory (1997–2002) – was one such research project that created a gateway of academic resources on the German web. GERHARD was a database-driven robot that collected academically relevant documents, which were indexed using computer-linguistic and statistical methods and classified by UDC. GERHARD's architecture consisted of a database-driven gatherer, automatic classification and an integrated searching and browsing service. The generated metadata and index of documents were held in a database that, towards the end of the project, contained 1,300,000 records. Automatic classification was based on the UDC trilingual authority files from the ETH (Federal Institute of Technology) library in Zürich, containing around 70,000 classes. This authority file supported searching of compound and complex UDC numbers and around 15 different relationships that can be established between individual UDC numbers (Möller et al., 1999). The gateway was taken down in 2006, following a shortage of funding.

In the USA, OCLC's research on the potentials of DDC use on the web was linked to a number of other projects on cataloguing of web resources that started in the early 1990s. Scorpion was one such project whose aim was to build tools for automatic subject assignment, combining automatic indexing techniques and DDC, and was envisaged as an aid to human cataloguing by automating subject assignment where items are available electronically. Scorpion was also used as an automatic classification tool in Renardus, a gateway to the cultural and scientific collections on the European web. The result of the project was an SG based on mapping different vocabularies and DDC with cross-SG browsing enabled through DDC (Koch, Neuroth and Day, 2003). The Renardus gateway was also taken down when funding ceased.

Similarly to SGs, digital repositories and open archives (learning materials, electronic journals, research papers and theses), which began appearing in greater numbers after 2000, also use bibliographic classifications. Committed to scholarly communication, by their very nature, repositories usually opt for bibliographic classifications that are widely used in national or international bibliographic services because the interoperability of subject access is an important requirement for their integration into national information networks (Koch, 2006).

The evolution of the web from purely academic to commercial, business and social coincided with a significant improvement in technology. Web portal developers started to be primarily interested in the benefits of concept organization into practical and purposeful categories that their users/customers could easily combine or independently navigate. Subject-orientated, simple hierarchical structures on gateways and portals have started to be combined with, or replaced by, a faceted organization of object/subject properties and attributes. These applications led to the development of data formats and tools for the management of faceted vocabularies and their use in a web interface (La Barre, 2006; Giess, Wild and McMahon, 2008).

Classification as a pivot and terminology services

The idea of using classification as a 'switching language' or 'pivot' to map indexing languages for the purpose of information integration and exchange was widely discussed in the 1970s (Marcella and Newton, 1994). This is even more relevant today, with the overall trend of information integration on the web. Classifications are particularly well suited for use as a central mapping spine in connecting the vocabularies of different languages and seem to give visible results quickly and easily.

In 1999 OCLC started the CORC (Cooperative Online Resource Catalog) project to provide tools for the co-operative creation, maintenance and use of metadata for web resources, which uses previous project material such as a tool for automatic classification developed in Scorpion. The goal of the project was to support access control for names or classification numbers in cases where different content can be supplied for different types of user (e.g. the meaning of a classification number could be given in different languages, or related to different user ages or educational levels). CORC also explores XML/RDF architecture in order to enable access and make use of existing authority files rather than creating new authority records. CORC records link DDC numbers with LCSH and this linking gathers a number of related subject headings under one classification number (Hickey and Vizine-Goetz, 1999). Since 2003, OCLC developments have been moving towards terminological services that provide shareable vocabulary data using open vocabulary encoding standards, XML and web services. Within these initiatives there are a number of significant developments in vocabulary mapping, e.g. DDC and LCSH, LCC, National Library of Medicine Classification (NLM) and DDC (Vizine-Goetz et al., 2004).

In Europe, examples of classification use in such contexts are also numerous. Concordances between DDC and UDC were prepared for the Czech Uniform Information Gateway in order to make it interoperable with gateways using DDC. The MSAC (Multilingual Subject Access to Catalogues of National

Libraries) project focused on mapping subject-heading systems in seven central European countries through UDC (Balikova, 2005). HILT (High-Level Thesaurus) was a UK project focused on linking subject vocabularies across a range of communities and services to support subject cross-searching and browsing. In its latest phase in 2009, it provided facilities for searching 11 subject vocabularies linked through a DDC outline, and machine-to-machine (m2m) pilot testing on several SGs. At the moment the European Library and Europeana projects are focusing on interoperability and mapping between vocabularies.

Classification for computers

According to Soergel (1999, 1119) classification can have many functions in information retrieval: providing semantic road maps; improving communication and learning; providing a conceptual base for the design of research; providing classification for actions; supporting information retrieval; providing a conceptual basis for knowledge-based systems; providing the conceptual basis for data element definition and object hierarchies in software systems; cross-discipline, cross-language and cross-culture mapping; and serving as a base for natural-language processing. This list of applications implies a strong relationship between classification and computers.

From the overview of classification use in library systems and on the web it is evident that, in spite of the fact that the intellectual content of a classification may be useful, there is very little use for it in information retrieval unless its content is machine readable and distributed in some kind of standardized format that can be automatically ingested and processed by information systems. From the use of classification on the web, however, it is obvious that domain-specific standards such as MARC are of little value once classification starts to be shared outside a specific domain. Standards are vehicles for KOS implementation and sharing, as recent developments can illustrate. For instance, ISO/IEC 13250 Topic Maps, BS 8723 Structured vocabularies for information retrieval and Simple Knowledge Organization System (SKOS) have all been created to support sharing and use of subject vocabularies across systems and domains. The general idea behind these and other such standards is that the availability and exchange of controlled vocabularies of various kinds and subject indexing languages in an open networked environment may contribute to resource discovery through referencing, resolving language ambiguities and providing a semantic context for text processing. With vocabularies expressed in a standardized way, there is a realistic prospect of centrally managed vocabulary repositories and services that will facilitate cross-collection resource discovery through vocabulary mappings and translation (Tudhope, Koch and Heery, 2006).

Through the use of an XML/RDF encoding schema that allow unique identification of data elements via a uniform resource identifier (URI), and their automatic linking and referencing on the open web, standards such as SKOS enable a more advanced way of processing semantics. Furthermore, indexing languages published in this way can then be combined and extended with various machine-understandable statements or inference rules using a formal web ontology language such as OWL (Web Ontology Language). Such an approach can lead to m2m processing of semantics captured in indexing languages and is considered one of the building blocks of the semantic web. With the advancement of XML/RDF technology, and the wider application of SKOS in publishing and linking subject vocabularies and document metadata, we can see how part of the semantic web scenario is unfolding. Currently, thesauri, classifications and collection metadata are released as SKOS data and are open for m2m processing and linking. The more data is published in this way, the greater the chance and incidence it has of being meaningfully and usefully connected. For example, connecting geodata to Wikipedia, library collections, or archival or museum collections looks very appealing from the point of view of the research and academic community.

However, for this scenario to work, both library collection metadata and KOSs should be published on the web as free and open for automatic processing and semantic linking. The publishing of library catalogues as linked data is supported through initiatives such as the W3C Library Linked Data Incubator Group (LLD XG). The publishing of bibliographic classifications schemes as linked data using SKOS XML/RDF is confronted with two obstacles. The first is that the SKOS data encoding model itself is not entirely suited to encoding the richness of semantic relationships and the structural complexity of universal classification, as we described above. The second, and probably more problematic, is related to the issue of copyright and restrictions imposed by publishers and owners of classification systems.

Brickley (2009) suggests that hybrid approaches may be the correct way to proceed: human classification mixed with automatic classification, professional subject schemes mixed with semi-structured user tagging, thing-oriented ontologies mixed with perspective and discipline-oriented subject classifications. In his opinion, the most pressing issue is that of sharing vocabularies on the open web:

By sharing what we know on the Web, by publishing every major classification system, thesaurus and subject headings system as a natural and essential part of the public information record, we open the door to the kind of hybrid models outlined above. There are all kinds of obstacles: cultural, technical, legal, practical. But the goal is inescapable. Subject classification systems and thesaurus systems which are not widely available in open formats will lose ground to those which are.

Conclusion

We have established that classifications are widely used in the bibliographic world, national bibliographies and library collections. From a more detailed analysis of some features of these systems it is evident that they have a very comprehensive vocabulary, structured and semantically related in the most intricate way, which is supported by natural-language terms in the form of subject–alphabetical indices. National SGs and portals organizing resources based on bibliographic classification have been continuously appearing since 2000, particularly in Central and Eastern Europe. As SGs evolved from simple directories to subject-oriented hub services, they started to use classification in a more sophisticated way: as a source of vocabulary for automatic classification and finally as a method of controlling and linking subject vocabularies behind the system. In this context, subject vocabularies started to be managed as authority tools and shared between metadata repositories in which classification was used as a means of semantic control. As SGs are established as academic research projects with no long-term funding or adequate business model, similar to many other web services, they tend to have a short life span, but it is not easy to predict when and if bibliographic classifications will cease to be used in this way.

In spite of the intensive use of classifications on the web there are relatively few studies measuring or assessing their usefulness in supporting information browsing. Vickery (2008, 3) concluded that online retrieval on the internet has 'largely done away with the need to mechanize sequential spatial display, but that the search result display could be considerably improved if systematic browsing options were provided'. Soergel (2009) reminds us that we have never actually seen a proper implementation of knowledge classification in a modern information retrieval system. One can only hope that such solutions will emerge with the wider use of classification schemes online. The increasing trend of sharing of KOSs on the web will influence the way we use classification systems in resource discovery in the future: hopefully as a source of complex concept relationships and an intricate interplay of subjects on which it would be possible to compute and mine for information and knowledge.

Acknowledgement

All copyright rights in the examples of DDC in this chapter are owned by OCLC Online Computer Library Center, Inc. ('OCLC') and used with permission. DDC, Dewey and Dewey Decimal Classification are registered trademarks/ service marks of OCLC.

References

Balikova, M. (2005) Multilingual Subject Access to Catalogues of National Libraries (MSAC): Czech Republic's collaboration with Slovakia, Slovenia, Croatia, Macedonia, Lithuania and Latvia, paper presented at *Libraries – A voyage of discovery, 71st IFLA General Conference and Council, 14–18 August 2005, Oslo, Norway*, http://archive.ifla.org/IV/ifla71/papers/044e-Balikova.pdf.

Bhattacharyya, G. (1979) Fundamentals of Subject Indexing Languages. In Neelameghan, A. (ed.), *Ordering Systems for Global Information Networks: proceedings of the Third International Study Conference on Classification Research held at Bombay, India, during 6–11 January 1975*, DRTC: FID/CR and Sarada Ranganathan Endowment for Library Science (FID 533), 83–99.

Brickley, D. (2009) Open Web Standards and Classification: foundations for a hybrid approach, keynote address at *Classification at the Crossroad: multiple directions to usability, International UDC Seminar 2009, 29–30 October 2009*, www.slideshare.net/danbri/open-web-standards-and-classication-foundations-for-a-hybrid-approach.

Broughton, V. (2004) *Essential Classification*, Facet Publishing.

Broughton, V. and Slavic, A. (2007) Building a Faceted Classification for the Humanities: principles and procedures, *Journal of Documentation*, **63** (5), 727–54.

Casson, E., Fabrizzi, A. and Slavic, A. (2009) Subject Search in Italian OPACs: an opportunity in waiting? In *Proceedings of the IFLA 2009 Satellite Meeting 'Looking at the Past and Preparing for the Future', Florence, 20–21 August 2009* [in print, in IFLA Publication series], pre-print version, www.ifla2009satelliteflorence.it/meeting2/program/assets/CassonFabrizziSlavic.pdf.

Cochrane, P. A. and Markey, K. (1985) Preparing for the Use of Classification in Online Cataloging Systems and in Online Catalogs, *Information Technology and Libraries*, **4** (2), 91–111.

Giess, M. D., Wild, P. J. and McMahon, C. A. (2008) The Generation of Faceted Classification Schemes for Use in the Organisation of Engineering Design Documents, *International Journal of Information Management*, **28**, 379–90.

Gnoli, C. and Mei, H. (2006) Freely Faceted Classification for Web-based Information Retrieval, *New Review of Hypermedia and Multimedia*, **12** (1), 63–81.

Guenther, R. S. (1994) The Library of Congress Classification in the USMARC Format, *Knowledge Organization*, **21** (4), 199–202.

Hancock, M. (1987) Subject Searching Behaviour at the Library Catalogue and at the Shelves: implications for online interactive catalogues, *Journal of Documentation*, **43** (4), 303–21, www.emeraldinsight.com/10.1108/eb026813.

Hickey, T. B. and Vizine-Goetz, D. (1999) The Role of Classification in CORC. In McKenna, B. (ed.), *Proceedings of the 23rd International Online Information Meeting, London, 7–9 December 1999*, Learned Information Europe Ltd, 247–50.

Hildreth, Ch. R. (1991) End Users and Structured Searching of Online Catalogues:

recent research finding. In Fugmann, R. (ed.), *Tools for Knowledge Organization and the Human Interface: proceedings of 1st International ISKO Conference, Darmstadt, 14–17 August, 1990*, Vol. 2, Indeks Verlag (Advances in Knowledge Organization 2), 9–19.

Hjørland, B. (2006). Facet, Facet Analysis and the Facet-analytic Paradigm in Knowledge Organization (KO), www.db.dk/bh/facet_and_facet_analysis.htm.

Hutchins, W. J. (1975) *Languages of Indexing and Classification*, Peter Peregrinus.

Kerr, L. (2009) Intute: from a distributed network to a unified database – lessons learned, *Extensions and Corrections to the UDC*, **31**, 173–82.

Koch, T. (2006) Electronic Thesis and Dissertation Services: semantic interoperability, subject access, multilinguality, *E-Thesis Workshop, Amsterdam, 19–20 January 2006*, www.ukoln.ac.uk/ukoln/staff/t.koch/publ/e-thesis-200601.html.

Koch, T., Neuroth, H. and Day, M. (2003) Renardus: cross-browsing European subject gateways via a common classification system (DDC). In McIlwaine, I. C. (ed.), *Subject Retrieval in a Networked Environment: proceedings of the IFLA Satellite Meeting held in Dublin, OH, 14–16 August 2001*, K. G. Saur (UBCIM Publications – New Series 25), 25–33.

La Barre, K. (2006) The Use of Faceted Analytico-synthetic Theory as Revealed in the Practice of Website Construction and Design, PhD thesis, Indiana University, School of Library and Information Science, https://netfiles.uiuc.edu/klabarre/www/LaBarre_FAST.pdf

Langridge, D. W. (1989) *Subject Analysis: principles and procedures*, Bowker-Saur.

Larson, R. R. (1991) The Decline of Subject Searching: long-term trends and patterns of index use in an online catalog, *Journal of the American Society for Information Science and Technology*, **42** (3), 197–215.

Mandel, C. (1995) Change and Continuity in Subject Authority Control. In *The Future Is Now: reconciling change and continuity control, proceedings of the OCLC Symposium, ALA Annual Conference, June 23, 1995*, www.oclc.org/oclc/man/9391ausy/mandle.htm.

Marcella, R. and Newton, R. (1994) *A New Manual of Classification*, Gower.

Markey, K. (1986) Users and the Online Catalog: subject access problems. In Matthews, J. R. (ed.), *The Impact of Online Catalogs*, Neal-Schuman Publishers, 35–70.

Markey, K. (1996) Classification to the Rescue: handling the problems of too many and too few retrievals. In Green, R. (ed.), *Knowledge Organization and Change: proceedings of the Fourth International ISKO Conference, Washington DC, 15–18 July 1996*, Indeks Verlag (Advances in Knowledge Organization 5), 107–36.

Markey, K. (2006) Forty Years of Classification Online: final chapter of future unlimited? In Mitchell, J. S. and Vizine-Goetz, D. (eds), *Moving beyond the Presentation Layer: content and context in the Dewey Decimal Classification (DDC) System*, The Haworth Information Press, 1–63.

Markey, K. and Weller, M. S. (1996) Failure Analysis of Subject Searches in a Test of

New Design for Subject Access to Online Catalogs, *Journal of the American Society for Information Science*, **47** (7), 519–37.

Möller, G. et al. (1999) Automatic Classification of the World Wide Web using Universal Decimal Classification. In McKenna, B. (ed.), *23rd International Online Information Meeting, London, 7–9 December 1999: proceedings*, Learned Information Europe, 231–7.

Slavic, A. (2006) UDC in Subject Gateways: experiment or opportunity? *Knowledge Organization*, **33** (3–4), 67–85.

Slavic, A. (2008) Faceted Classification: management and use, *Axiomathes*, **18** (2), 257–71.

Slavic, A. and Cordeiro, M. I (2004) Sharing and Re-use of Classification Systems: the need for a common data model, *Signum*, **8**, 19–24, pre-print available at http://dlist.sir.arizona.edu/1274.

Soergel, D. (1999) The Rise of Ontologies or the Reinvention of Classification, *Journal of the American Society for Information Science*, **50** (12), 1119–20.

Svenonius, E. (1983) Use of Classification in Online Retrieval, *Library Resources and Technical Services*, **27** (1), 76–80.

Svenonius, E. (1997) Definitional Approaches in the Design of Classification and Thesauri and Their Implications for Retrieval and for Automatic Classification. In *Knowledge Organization for Information Retrieval: proceedings of the Sixth International Study Conference on Classification Research, London, 16–18 June 1997*, FID 716, 12–16.

Szostak, R. and Gnoli, C. (2008) Classifying by Phenomena, Theories and Methods: examples with focused social science theories. In *Culture and Identity in Knowledge Organization: proceedings of the Tenth International ISKO Conference, Montréal, 5–8 August 2008*, 203–9.

Tudhope, D., Koch, T. and Heery, R. (2006) Terminology Services and Technology: JISC state of the art review, www.ukoln.ac.uk/terminology/JISC-review2006.html.

Vickery, B. C. (2008) Faceted Classification for the Web, *Axiomathes*, **18** (2), 145–60.

Vizine-Goetz, D. et al. (2004) Vocabulary Mapping for Terminology Services, *Journal of Digital Information*, **4** (4), article 272.

Wajenberg, A. S. (1983) MARC Coding of DDC for Subject Retrieval, *Information Technology and Libraries*, **2** (3), 246–51.

Yu, H. and Young, M. (2004) The Impact of Web Search Engines on Subject Searching in OPAC, *Information Technology and Libraries*, **23** (4), 168–80.

3

·●·

Approaches to fiction retrieval research: from theory to practice?

Anat Vernitski and Pauline Rafferty

Introduction

This chapter considers fiction retrieval research and initiatives, providing an overview of some of the approaches that have been developed. In particular, it describes two recent approaches to fiction retrieval that have made use of theoretical concepts drawn from literary theory.

Fiction is an interesting information domain because it includes documents that serve two purposes, which are reading for pleasure and scholarly study (Beghtol, 1994, 3), but fiction retrieval has not always focused on both aspects. In the 19th century, the approach was to treat fiction from a knowledge perspective within general classification schemes. The Dewey Decimal Classification (DDC), the Library of Congress Classification (LCC) and the Universal Decimal Classification (UDC) contain classes for literature, with the main subdivision in each case being the language in which it is written. Further subdivision is possible based on literary form, historical period or the works of an individual author (Riesthuis, 1997).

It may be that there is a relationship between the development of literary studies as academic scholarship and approaches to fiction retrieval in libraries. In the UK, for example, Literary Studies as an academic discipline developed in the 19th century, institutionalized in the Mechanics' Institutes, working-men's colleges and extension lecturing circuits before its acceptance in the universities (Eagleton, 1996, 23). In its early days in the academy, English Studies was considered to be 'an upstart, amateurish affair as academic subjects went, hardly able to compete on equal terms with the rigours of Greats or philology' (Eagleton, 1996, 25). It is a relatively new academic discipline, although its research methods and interpretative approaches have a much longer history, at least since Aristotle's *Poetics*. We know that during the late 19th and early 20th centuries public libraries in England were still capping the number of novels that patrons were able to borrow, which suggests some nervousness about the role of the library and the librarian. There seemed to be concern, evidenced in the letters pages of the Library Association journal of the time, about whether libraries should be encouraging the reading of novels and the consumption of fiction for pleasure alone or whether they should be concerned with the intellectual 'improvement' of their patrons by encouraging the reading of serious, knowledge-based literature (Barr and Sturges, 1992).

In the 20th century, fiction retrieval designers have been more amenable to the idea of designing retrieval systems to facilitate access in relation to the cultural, leisure and pleasure aspects of fiction (e.g. Beghtol, 1989, 1990, 1994, 1995; Pejtersen, 1978, 1979, 1994; Saarti, 1999, 2000, 2002). Opportunities for innovative retrieval design have become possible in and through the web. Fiction retrieval is an area of information retrieval that demonstrates the interrelationships between information technology and information retrieval. Information retrieval design, which is ultimately about allowing people to choose the documents that most closely match their information wants, needs and desires from the possible range of documents (Warner, 2010), is highly dependent on specific information technologies to actualize theory. Indeed, fiction retrieval design is an excellent example of how developments in technology have facilitated designs that otherwise might well have remained theoretical.

Fiction retrieval asks questions about the nature of fictional documents; the relationships between fiction and knowledge organization; the status of the fictional document as individual entity and as part of a putative class (e.g. Beghtol, 1994); the 'aboutness' of the fictional document (Beghtol, 1994; Rafferty and Hidderley, 2005); and the challenge of the polysemic nature of fiction for information retrieval design. Many of these questions overlap with the kinds of questions asked by literary theorists about the nature of text and textuality, about genres and intertextuality, about separateness and interconnections. Indeed, some of these questions have sometimes taken concrete form through information technologies. One of the most interesting aspects of information technology development, in the form of the web in particular, is the way in which these discourses, which were previously separate, coalesce. We find too that some recent approaches to fiction retrieval have borrowed from literary theory to explore aspects of fiction information retrieval. The creative coalescence of discourses perhaps offers the most potential for developing fiction retrieval research. With that in mind, after a brief overview of some fiction retrieval solutions, this chapter will explore two approaches to fiction retrieval, which have developed from the literary theory concepts of intertextuality and genres. It is hoped that these approaches may offer some ideas for further research in the field.

Approaches to fiction retrieval

The most comprehensive overview of fiction information retrieval from its initial emergence until 1994 is probably Beghtol's *The Classification of Fiction* (1994), based on her PhD thesis. Beghtol addresses theoretical issues relating to fiction knowledge organization, including questions about fiction as a discursive regime, and, citing Immroth, argues that traditional subdivisions for fiction sometimes do not work even for the literary scholar because of the following requirements of such scholars:

> I want a book on man's inhumanity to man, or perhaps, more precisely, a work of English literature, or something from the eighteenth century on man's inhumanity to man . . . Our present approaches within subject analyses, within classification schemes in particular and lists of subject headings also, will probably be of little use to me.
> (Immroth, 1974, 257)

Beghtol notes that fiction retrieval-system design in the 20th century includes the adaptation of existing classification schemes to deal with fiction and the creation of special classification schemes for fiction. An example of the adaptation of general classification schemes is to be found in Haigh's 1933 adaptation of DDC3 (originally published in 1888), which preserved main class headings but replaced subdivisions with notations indicating genre and form (Sapp, 1986). The internal logic of Haigh's classification scheme has been criticized (Pejtersen and Austin 1983; Sapp 1986; Beghtol, 1989). Not the least of its problems was the fact that the source classification scheme was itself already 40 years out of date at the time it was adapted.

In general, the development of special schemes has been theoretical rather than practical. In 1936, Burgess published a hierarchical decimal classification scheme for fiction in which the main classes were a combination of genres and literary styles (Pejtersen and Austin, 1983). Walker's 'Problem Child' faceted classification scheme for fiction (1970) was developed as part of a Strathclyde University MA thesis (Beghtol, 1994). There are three facets in the system: author, narrative and subject, and it has a non-hierarchical, mixed, partially retroactive notation (Beghtol, 1994, 59). Beghtol suggests that the facet formula for this system is a variation of Ranganathan's PMEST, $PM_{(PMEST)}E(ST)$ (Figure 3.1 overleaf). While the designs are innovative and creative, there are no recorded examples of the implementation of either scheme, although it is possible that Walker's scheme was implemented at a local level in Lanarkshire libraries.

Cameron's 1952 Fantasy Classification System (FCS) has a hierarchical notation and is intended for use within a classified catalogue (Beghtol, 1994). There are two parts to this system. One is a subject classification and the other

P		= Author/title cataloguing
M(PMEST)		= Subject of the novel
P		= Characters of the novel
M		= Kind of life portrayed
E		= Theme(s)
S		= Geographic setting
T		= Setting in time
E		= Narrative type of the novel
(ST)		= Language and time period of the author

Figure 3.1 *Facet formula for Walker's 'Problem Child' system (Beghtol, 1994, 61)*

is the 'Literary Information Profile' (Figure 3.2). Each part has a different notation so that each fictional work receives two notations: one is numeric, to describe content, and one is alphabetic, to describe attributes. The notation could be extremely unwieldy and complex (Figure 3.3). In addition, there is no preferred citation order, which makes the scheme unsuitable for filing purposes. However, any classification scheme that begins with a main class named 'Aberrations' is certainly worthy of attention!

Main classes of the Fantasy Classification System
00 Aberrations
10 Supernatural beings
20 Extrapolations on life and mind
30 Extrapolations on living
40 Supernatural places and things
50 Extrapolations on space
60 Extrapolations on technology
70 The past
80 Extrapolations on time
90 Supernatural, Unrationalised and Distorted powers and themes
Literary Information Profile
Length (e.g. short-short)
type of plot (e.g. war)
appeal (e.g. intellectual)
stress (e.g. personalities, psychology)
fantastic orientation (e.g. fantasy dominant)
subsidiary considerations (e.g. story associated with series)

Figure 3.2 *Cameron's Fantasy Classification Scheme (Beghtol, 1994, 48–9)*

van Voght, A. E. Slan
22.5,1+ (31.8:52.8:36.7): 34.2+ 65.2 dbudbh

Figure 3.3 *Example of FCS notation (Beghtol, 1994, 51)*

Other fiction retrieval researchers have made creative use of information technologies to develop interesting systems, following the approach initiated by Annelise Pejtersen's Bookhouse system, which is of interest not only because of its use of IT but also because of its move towards user warrant rather than literary warrant as its design foundation (Pejtersen, 1978, 1989; Pejtersen and Austin, 1983, 1984). Underpinning the Bookhouse system is a multi-dimensional indexing system called the Analysis and Mediation of Publications (AMP) system. AMP is built on the four dimensions through which users sub-consciously classify fiction: subject matter, frame, author's intention and accessibility (Figure 3.4). A framework for subject analysis was developed for the project and a thesaurus of controlled terms and rules for indexing was developed to ensure a consistent and suitable vocabulary and to reduce, as far as possible, the subjectivity of judgements within categories such as 'author intentions' (Pejtersen and Austin, 1984). Another fiction database developed from the principle of user warrant is EDVIN, a subject-term and genre database for fiction and biographies developed for use in Swedish public libraries (Ekvall and Larsson, 1997).

Analysis and Mediation of Publications (AMP)
1. Subject matter
a. action and course of events
b. psychological development and description
c. social relations
2. Frame: setting
a. time: past, present, future
b. place: geographical, social environment, profession
3. Author's intentions
a. emotional experience
b. cognition and information
4. Accessibility
a. readability
b. physical characteristics, literary form

Figure 3.4 *Pejtersen's AMP categories (Pejtersen, 1989)*

In the UK, The Society of Chief Librarians' initiative, Branching Out, played an important role in developing innovative 'reader development' projects within public libraries in England and Wales between 1999 and 2001. One of the Branching Out projects was the development of a fiction retrieval system, 'Whichbook', now managed by Opening the Book (www.whichbook.net/). The philosophy underpinning the system is that as the 'subject approach' to fiction is multi-dimensional and fiction retrieval systems should allow readers to search for fiction using 'affective dimension' searching (e.g. searching for happy or sad books) rather than confining searches to known-item searching or to genre-based searching. There is also a Norwegian version called Ønskebok.no, which was launched in 2007. Opening the Book manages other reader development-orientated websites such as 'Reader 2 Reader' and 'Scottish Readers', which make use of affective-dimension user tagging of books to facilitate access (www.openingthebook.com/).

Intertextuality and fiction information retrieval

Anat Vernitski's prototype fiction retrieval system was developed from an MSc dissertation undertaken at City University, London, in 2007. Vernitski argued that while there are specialist fiction retrieval systems for reading for pleasure, some of which are used in public libraries, scholars who read fiction as a professional pursuit have not had a specialist classification scheme to correspond to their information needs. Research shows that scholars in the humanities tend to use specific search terms rather than general concepts (Buchanan, 2005, 219). In particular, the intertextual approach to the study of fiction, which looks at the interrelations between primary literary texts, is not catered for in any of the existing classification and fiction retrieval schemes. The identification of this gap led to the proposal of a classification scheme that uses categories inspired by the research involved in fiction retrieval systems. Secondary and tertiary documents provide an objective framework for deciding on intertextual links between primary fiction documents, in a form that libraries and information professionals could use without having to conduct their own fiction scholarly research.

The notion of 'intertextuality' derives from Julie Kristeva's work. Kristeva (1986 [1966]) argued that literary texts contain elements transported from other texts. In this context, 'transported' means that not only does a literary text use elements from other texts, for example in the form of quotations or parody, but the elements of a literary text that originated in previous literary texts are changed as they are transported into the new text because they are understood differently in the context of the new text. The term, 'intertextuality' might be a relatively new one, but the practice of intertextuality in fiction is not; for example, the plot of *Hamlet* is based on a Scandinavian story of family feud, first recorded in the 12th century by Saxo Grammaticus in his *Historia Danica*, while the English play that Shakespeare most probably used as his source for the play was Thomas Kyd's *Spanish Tragedy* (Hubler, 1987, 183–4).

Intertextuality is already recognized within the literature of information science (Rowley and Farrow, 2000, 42). In their discussion of the links between documents, Rowley and Farrow use the term to denote the interrelations between documents, 'from the tracking down of passing allusions to full-blown parody', arguing that it is not only literary scholars who may be interested in relationships between documents, because 'a user who is interested in one [document] may well be interested in the other also' (2000, 42). Researchers of fiction retrieval systems have also recognized the value of an intertextuality-oriented classification scheme. Ranta (1991) describes a system for indexing fiction in a scholarly academic environment, arguing that fiction should be classified to allow for various approaches used by scholars to study literature (Saarti, 1999, 88).

Research conducted into information seeking by humanities scholars shows that chaining, defined as following citations and references in known documents in order to discover new documents, is their most common search strategy (Buchanan, 2005, 225). The practice of chaining is similar in principle to the intertextual principle of linking works of fiction, yet used in a wider scholarly context. The fact that chaining is so central to the information needs of humanities scholars suggests that the development of an intertextual classification scheme would probably be useful to scholars studying fiction, even if they have not used intertextual research before. Intertextuality, then, seems to capture an essential aspect of information needs in the humanities.

A prerequisite to the development of the intertextual scheme was the development of suitable categories. Beghtol's Experimental Fiction Analysis System (EFAS) (Beghtol, 1994, 178) and the 1998 Functional Requirements for Bibliographic Records IFLANET report were used as a starting point for choosing categories. The EFAS classes were of interest because they are the most detailed among fiction retrieval systems. The EFAS classes, which are four basic, fiction-specific major data elements: time, space, event and character, and one general data element (Other), might allow for an intertextual link to be made between two books when they refer to the same character or event, or when they describe a narrative that is located in the same time or the same space. However, this set of classes does not cover a number of common intertextual links between texts. For example, if one text contains a quotation from another text, this link cannot be represented using EFAS classes. Moreover, the categories of character, event, time and space can appear in intertextual links as a cluster of categories and cannot always be well differentiated (Vernitski, 2007).

Another possible source for categories for an intertextuality-based fiction classification scheme is the Functional Requirements for Bibliographic Records (FRBR) model, which grew out of the work of the IFLA Standing Committee on Cataloguing, which resulted from the 1990 IFLA Stockholm Seminar on Bibliographic Records (Plassard, 1998). The Stockholm Seminar emphasized the need to develop universal cataloguing rules for bibliographic records that would serve to describe not only works but also relationships between works. The entities studied were Work, Expression (revisions of the original text, for example abridgement or musical accompaniment), Manifestation (the physical form of a text, for example a specific edition), Item (a single physical object representing a particular manifestation of a work, for example a physical single book in a library) and Person (corresponding to the category of responsibility in AACR2).

FRBR defines various types of relationships between Work and Manifestation, Work and Expression, and Work and Person. Examples of such types are the relationships of Work to Expression and Expression to Manifestation, Work to Expression and Expression to Item, Person to Works, Person to Expressions, Person to Manifestations, Person to Items, Subject to Works, Manifestation to other Manifestations, and Work to Work. It seems that the relationship of Work to Work is the most relevant for an intertextuality-oriented fiction classification scheme. The relationship of Work to Work includes the following types of relationships: Adaptation, Sequel of, Supplement of, Musical Setting of, Paraphrase, Dramatisation, and Part to Whole. Of these categories, the categories of Supplement of, Musical Setting of, Dramatisation, and Part to Whole are not relevant to the representation of intertextual relationships. The remaining categories also have their limitations. The categories of Adaptation and Paraphrase may overlap in most cases and the differentiation between them is not entirely clear. Furthermore, the cases of quotations and of similarities in titles cannot be represented by these categories. Neither the EFAS nor the FRBR model was entirely suitable for an intertextuality-based classification scheme, so a customized set of categories is used to create the scheme, based on EFAS and FRBR.

The categories proposed in the intertextual scheme are: Quotation, Allusion and Adaptation (Vernitski, 2007). The Quotation category is divided into the categories of Exact Quotation and Misquotation, as a misquotation used in a work is often recognizable and thus creates an intertextual link to another work. The Allusion category is divided into the categories of Title Allusion and Name Allusion. Title Allusions can be allusions to the Title of a Work, and Title of a Chapter or Section. Name Allusions can be allusions to the names of a Character, Place, Institution and Concept. The Adaptation category is divided into adaptations of the Same Theme in a Different Form and adaptation of the Same Form with a Different Theme. Finally, another category is Sequel of, as sometimes works are written as sequels to other works, either by the same author or by a different author (usually as a tribute). The categories and sub-categories are shown in Figure 3.5 overleaf.

The notation chosen for the intertextuality-oriented classification scheme uses the first letter of the main class name to represent main classes. Sub-classes are represented by the first letter of the main class name separated by a slash from the first letters of the sub-class name. The notations are shown in Figure 3.6 overleaf.

As Saarti explains, when a librarian assigns fiction categories there is a problem of subjectivity, which stems from each person's own interpretation of the work of fiction (Saarti 1999, 90–1). The use of a scholarly article as a source

Quotation
Exact Quotation
Misquotation
Allusion
Title
Work title
Chapter/section title
Name
Character
Place
Institution
Concept
Variation
Theme
Form
Sequel

Quotation	Q
Exact Quotation	Q/Ex
Misquotation	Q/Mis
Allusion	**A**
Title	A/T
-Title of Work	A/T/Wor
-Title of a Section or Chapter in a work	A/T/Sec
Name	A/N
-Character Name	A/N/Cha
-Place Name	A/N/Pla
-Institution Name	A/N/Ins
-Concept Name	A/N/Con
Variation	**V**
Theme	V/Th
Form	V/Fo
Sequel	**S**

Figure 3.5

Categories in Vernitski's fiction intertextuality-orientated classification

Figure 3.6

Notations in Vernitski's fiction intertextuality-orientated classification

for intertextuality-oriented fiction classification ensures that there is continuity in the use of the scheme in different libraries, and the system promises to be as universal as possible. Each work of fiction is identified by its author and title. Other bibliographical data are not included in the index, because the index is designed to be used in conjunction with a library catalogue. It is envisaged that each library should customize the index so that works mentioned in the index, if they are available at the specific library, may be linked, by the use of hyperlink, to the record of the work in the library catalogue. Moreover, intertextual links exist between works, and not between their various expressions and manifestations, so other features of the work are not necessary in this index. Examples of intertextual links between works of fiction, and the sources used to establish these links are shown in Figure 3.7 overleaf.

Creating an index based on the intertextuality-oriented classification scheme requires specialist knowledge and would be expensive to implement in practice because the staff involved in scanning scholarship, identifying intertextual links and entering the information into the database should ideally have dual postgraduate education level in both literature and information studies. Web development staff would be required in order to develop the web-based display of the index and ensure its usability. Finally, administrative and marketing staff would be required in order to implement the project and bring it to the attention of potential users (Vernitski, 2007). The links would need to be accurate, precise and scholarly for such a system to be useful, and whereas affective dimension-type tagging is facilitated by Web 2.0 approaches, it is not at all clear that such

Work 1	Mary Shelley, *Frankenstein*
Work 2	Cornelius Agrippa, *Three Books of Occult Philosophy*
Type of link	Allusion–Character A/N/Cha
Source	David Margolies, 'From Social Bond to Contract: Debt in Rabelais and Shakespeare', *New Comparison*, 33–34 (Spring–Autumn 2002), 27–37
Note	In Frankenstein, Shelley mocks the figure of Cornelius Agrippa, who in the early 16th century developed scientific theories based on hypothesis without any empirical investigation.
Work 1	William Shakespeare, *King Lear*
Work 2	Francois Rabelais, *Gargantua and Pantagruel*
Type of link	Variation–Theme V/Th
Source	David Margolies, 'From Social Bond to Contract: Debt in Rabelais and Shakespeare', *New Comparison*, 33–34 (Spring–Autumn 2002), 27–37
Note	Both texts use the metaphor of debt to represent social relations.
Work 1	Francesco Petrarch, *Poetry*
Work 2	Edmund Spenser, *The Faerie Queene*
Type of link	Adaptation–Form V/Fo
Source	Joseph Parry, 'Petrarch's Mourning, Spenser's Scudamour, and Britomart's Gift of Death', *Comparative Literature Studies*, 42 (1) (2005), 24–49
Note	Spenser's use of the allegory of chastity is a reworking of Petrarch's use of this image in his love poetry.
Work 1	Jane Austen, *Northanger Abbey*
Work 2	Charles Dickens, *Dombey and Son*
Type of link	Allusion–Concept A/N/Con
Source	Ephraim Sicher, 'A Waste of Money? Recycling and the Economy of Our Mutual Friend', *New Comparison*, 33–34 (Spring–Autumn 2002), 131–41
Note	The dangers of commercialism are discussed in both these novels; Austen laments the publications of cheap anthologies and Dickens shows how Dombey's son questions the value of money.
Work 1	Tatsuzo Ishikawa, *Ikiteru heitai* [Living Soldiers]
Work 2	Dalton Trumbo, *Johnny Got His Gun*
Type of link	Allusion–Place A/N/Pl
Source	Jonathan E. Abel, 'Canon and Censor: How War Wounds Bodies of Writing', *Comparative Literature Studies*, 42 (1) (2005), 74–93
Note	The common place described in these novels is the battleground, focusing on wounded soldiers.
Work 1	Lope de Vega, *La fingido verdadero* [The True Pretender]
Work 2	Jean Rotron, *La veritable Saint Genest* [The True St. Genesius]
Type of link	Allusion–Institution A/N/Inst
Source	Barbara Simerka, 'Metatheatre and Scepticism in Early Modern Representations of the Saint Genesius Legend', *Comparative Literature Studies*, 42 (1) (2005), 50–73
Note	Both plays use the institution of the theatre as a metaphor for scepticism that is expressed in doubts and regrets.
Work 1	Karen Joy Fowler, *The Jane Austen Club*
Work 2	Jane Austen, *Emma*
Type of link	Allusion–Character A/N/Cha
Source	Patricia T. O'Conner, '"The Jane Austen Book Club": Mr Darcy Is a Boorish Snob. Please Discuss', *New York Times*, 2 May 2004.
Note	The character Jocelyn in Fowler's novel is a matchmaker and a control freak, based on Austen's Emma.
Work 1	George Gordon Byron, *Manfred*
Work 2	Ivan Turgenev, *Steno*
Type of link	Variation–Form V/Fo
Source	L. A. Balykova (ed.), *Biblioteka Ivana Sergeevicha Turgeneva: Chast' 1: knigi na russkom iazyke* [The Library of Ivan Sergeevich Turgenev: Part 1: Books in Russian], izd. OGTRK: Orel, 1994
Note	Turgenev was influenced by Byron's play *Manfred* when he wrote his own first play, *Steno*.

Figure 3.7 *Examples of Vernitski's fiction intertextuality-orientated classification*

systems will ever be able to generate scholarly information retrieval systems. The work on this project has generated some ideas for further research. The classification system itself might be refined. The fact that chaining, which resembles intertextual research in its approach to documentation, is widely used in humanities research means that this project might be used as an initial structure on which later research into information systems incorporating chaining could be used by the humanities scholarly community at large. Furthermore, the intertextuality-oriented project might yield interest in the area of the links between scholarly studies of literature and librarianship studies, and it could be useful to conduct theoretical research of this sort because it might result in further joint projects across the multi-disciplinary board (Vernitski, 2007). Finally, the area of specialist classification research might benefit from the work done in this project, in developing new ideas about specialist classification and its uses, thus contributing to information studies research.

A methodological framework for a generic fiction retrieval system

In general, models of fiction indexing lack much in the way of historicity. Where genre is invoked, the notion of genre is often ontological. Saarti (2000) and Vernitski (2007) both favour Beghtol's EFAS model as a foundation for fiction indexing, Saarti relating the EFAS model to Ranganathan's PMEST formula; but what might be needed to enrich descriptions of fictional works is the inclusion of some notion of historicity in the fiction-description model. A prototype project has been undertaken to explore the development of a generic knowledge-organization tool for fiction (Rafferty, 2008, 2009, 2010). In this project, the inclusion of historicity is at the level of genre history and the web of textuality within which individual works reside. Recent literary-critical approaches to genre theory emphasize genre as classification, with the attendant problems of establishing the constitution of the 'class' and of unit members within the class (e.g. Dowd, Stevenson and Strong, 2006; Fowler, 1982; Frow, 2006). Frow (2006) uses the concept of schema to explore generic systems. To speak of schema is to assume that knowledge is organized, so that knowledge about a specific domain is not knowledge as unconnected facts but knowledge that coheres in specifiable ways.

Genres act as the cues that enable us to interpret the knowledge in relation to the relevant domain. However, genre is not only an already existing set of concepts and their relationships but also an operative function, which, in the right context, activates the relevant conceptual meaning. The perception of concepts as coherent wholes can operate at different levels of comprehension. Frow argues that at the level of the generic frame these coherent wholes can be understood as 'projected worlds' (2006, 85), by which he means 'a relatively bounded and schematic domain of meanings, values and affects, accompanied by a set of instructions for handling them. Any world can be described through a coherent set of propositions, and generated reality-effects specific to it: some worlds claim a high reality status, others announce themselves as fictional or hypothetical' (2006, 86). Every genre is defined in part by the 'bounded province of meaning which is specific to it and which it makes available for use' (2006, 87). This view of genre is of the generic structure as a set of ontological boundaries within which any specific generic text might be recognized. But this view does not address the historicity of the bounded, conventional information domain which constitutes genre.

Genre can be seen as a set of conventions and rules about the discursive possibilities within specific information domains, which operate in and through institutionalized means of dissemination. However, the rules and conventions are not static, but are diachronically dynamic, determined in the last instance by the arbiters of authority within the specific domain in fiction: traditional publishers. Generic categorization in the historical context is more complex than the ontological schema or any notion of the novel as a pure, historically determined but ultimately individual unit can describe. Generic formation is the interplay of elements that are chosen, modified, critiqued, engaged with and manipulated by material, generically aware writers, in and through a specific historical context (Rafferty, 2010).

A key assumption in this approach to genre is that literary genres are constructed in and through the writings of individual authors, who use the codes and conventions of the genre and thus, in some way, but not necessarily the 'received way', perpetuate the genre. Genre, viewed diachronically, is dialogic, in that there are relationships between texts written at an earlier date and texts written at a later date, and dialectic, in that instantiations of structural codes and conventions in individual texts may over time change generic codes and conventions at the structural level. When a genre no longer ideologically fits with a society it may wither away or become substantially transformed. Producers of generic cultural products are themselves, at some level, already consumers of the generic cultural products the production of which they are contributing to. This means that in popular culture consumption is always a prerequisite of popular culture production.

The methodological framework for the generic knowledge organization tool enables intertextual connections in and through a large data set of genre novels in the form of generic codes and conventions to be identified. Specific texts are mapped out in relation to the generic codes and conventions, themselves the product of specific concrete texts. The initial set of generic codes and conventions (plot, theme, characters) is constructed through reference to pre-texts and literary criticism and history. This framework has the flexibility to allow cultural artefacts to be considered as the products of human agency, but also recognizes that those human agents always work within the possibilities and limitations of existing societal constructs and constraints. The framework has been piloted using Northern Irish Troubles genre novels (Rafferty, 2008, 2009) and the approach consisted of the following steps:

- The characteristics of the genre were identified using literary history and criticism.
- A representative data set was acquired for the pilot exercise.
- Texts were described and coded using data-gathering sheets designed for the study.
- Texts were sorted into historical order and pre-texts were identified.
- Syntagms (narrative chains) and paradigms (dominant genre type, characters) were identified within the initial historically organized subset of novels. In the case of Troubles fiction, this was the subset of novels published in 1969 and 1970.
- Using the historical framework, each novel was coded as a replication novel, a modification novel or a challenging novel against an initial set of generic codes and conventions. A picture of small transformations emerges from this analysis, which provides a rich diachronic analysis and describes the micro-history of the genre.
- Data was input into a primary sources database.

This approach is concerned with the production of genre novels by authors-as-producers in relation to the consumption of genre novels, either specifically (reading concrete texts) or generally (awareness of codes and conventions as a result of general circulation of the genre). To map out material instances of intertextuality, analytical concepts drawn from semiotics, specifically, paradigms and syntagms that have their origins in Saussurean linguistics, were used. For the Saussurean linguists, meaning in language is constructed through difference, so that signifiers only have meaning relative to other signifiers, present or absent. The construction of meaning is governed by operations on two planes, the paradigmatic and the syntagmatic.

Paradigms refer to the choice of specific signifiers in opposition to other possible signifiers. Within critical theory frameworks, the choice of specific signifiers involves ideological implications. Syntagms are the combinations or chains of elements which form a meaningful whole within a text. In this project, paradigmatic choice relates to the types of characters included in the novel, in particular to choices about characters. Identifying the syntagmatic axis in this study takes the form of identifying the chains of signifiers that contribute to making meaning within the novels. In relation to popular culture novels, syntagmatic combinations refer to plot and narrative. Following the Russian Formalists, it is possible to suggest that plot and narrative are not necessarily the same. The plot is the story; the narrative is the way in which the story is told. The range and types of plots circulating in novels at any synchronic moment is of interest, as are the transformations in plots over time. Genre is determined by both paradigmatic selections and syntagmatic combinations.

A summary plot synopsis was constructed for each novel in the pilot set. Initial categories were developed from pre-texts and the secondary literature. Paradigmatic choices that authors make regarding the representation of heroes, villains and female characters were then recorded. Wherever possible, modality markers were established and identified. These include reference to the material world (places, people, institutions, events).

Evidence of ideological stance might be drawn from the plot, from representations of characters, or from clues in the narrative or style of discourse. It is in relation to ideology that Stuart Hall's encoding/decoding model becomes particularly useful, as it was originally designed to map ideological reception positions. Hall's communication model is of particular use to this project because it emphasizes active reception. The approach adopted in this study is to take empirical data – in the pilot this data takes the form of descriptions of Troubles Fiction novels – and read this data against a novel adaptation of Stuart Hall's encoding/decoding model to analyse specific diachronic transformations emerging in and through genres.

Hall (2001) distinguished between three theoretically possible decoding positions. These are the following:

- Dominant-hegemonic position: 'When the viewer takes the connoted meaning from, say, a television newscast or current affairs programme full and straight, and decodes the message in terms of the reference code in which it has been encoded, we might say that the viewer is operating inside the dominant code' (Hall, 2001, 174).
- Negotiated code or position: 'Decoding within the negotiated version contains a mixture of adaptive and oppositional elements: it acknowledges the legitimacy of the hegemonic definitions to make the grand significations (abstract), while, at a more restricted, situational (situated) level, it makes its own ground rules – it operates with exceptions to the rule. It accords the privileged position to the dominant definitions of events while reserving the right to make a more negotiated application to local conditions, to its own more corporate positions' (Hall, 2001, 175).
- Oppositional code: 'Finally it is possible for a viewer perfectly to understand both the literal and the connotative inflection given by a discourse but to decode the message in a globally contradictory way.

He/she detotalizes the message in the preferred code in order to retotalize the message within some alternative framework of reference. This is the case of the viewer who listens to a debate on the need to limit wages but "reads" every mention of "national interest" as "class interest"' (Hall, 2001, 175).

Hall's model was used as a starting point to construct a framework within which three categories are used to describe the relationship of specific novels to earlier novels. These categories are:

- Replication: this category is used to describe specific novels which adhere closely to the conventions of the genre identified through an examination of the earliest texts. (An example of this category, drawn from the Troubles fiction study, is Tom Clancy's *Patriot Games*, 1987.)
- Modification: this category is used to describe specific novels that generally adhere to the conventions of the genre identified through an examination of the earliest texts, but display specific differences. (An example would be Gerald Seymour's *Field of Blood*, 1985. The plot of this novel concerns the IRA supergrass trials of the 1980s. There are some low-level changes in the codes and conventions used in the representation of paramilitary characters in this book.)
- Challenge: this category is used to describe specific novels that do not adhere to the conventions of the genre but construct alternative representations. Within this category are also included novels that critique conventional representations. It is expected that in most genres this category will be much smaller than the other two. (An example is Robert McLiam Wilson's *Ripley Bogle*, 1989. This is a meta-fiction that is, arguably, as much a commentary on Troubles fiction as a Troubles novel.) (Rafferty, 2009).

A data-gathering instrument that includes fields for recording bibliographic information and content description was developed. This forms the record for the fiction knowledge-organization system and will include information recorded at the level of denotation (bibliographic, character identification, plot summary, modality markers) and connotation (ideology markers, categorization). Table 3.1 overleaf shows the data categories included in the fictional knowledge tool.

It might be possible to implement such a system through a user-based website, with reader ratings forming the interpretative analytical activity that assigns each novel a 'relation to generic conventions' position. The status of each novel as interpreted by the community of readers would be open to

Table 3.1 *Categories in the data-gathering sheets*

Category	Description and function
Bibliographic information	Author, title, publisher, date of publication, place, language
Dominant affective genre	The dominant genre type that best describes the novel.
Plot summary label	
Representations of key characters	Paradigmatic choices about heroes, villains and female characters.
Modality markers	These might include reference to the material world (places, people, institutions, events).
Ideology stance	This is related to positive, neutral or negative attitudes. Evidence might come from the plot, characters or clues in the narrative or style of discourse.
Relation to genre conventions	Replicate, modify, challenge.

historical shifts and alterations over time. Hidderley and Rafferty's work on the notion of democratic indexing (e.g. Hidderley and Rafferty, 1997; Rafferty and Hidderley, 2005, 2007) offers an approach to recording any such interpretative transformations through the process of reconciliation. This process examines the terms or tags attached to each field and creates a collective interpretation for each field based on counting of terms. It is acknowledged that interpretation changes over time, so this would have to be an iterative process.

Conclusion

Recent innovations in tagging and Web 2.0 approaches to information retrieval open the door for affective-dimension indexing, which could potentially allow for the development of interesting approaches to the retrieval of cultural documentation, including fiction. Indeed, recent developments in the semantic web (Web 3.0) and even the social semantic web, might suggest scope for combining elements of controlled vocabulary systems with tagging and other user-generated indexing initiatives. There are issues, however, about user tagging when users undertake the tagging without referential guidelines and frameworks, and certainly it is highly unlikely that Web 2.0 approaches could be used to actualize Vernitski's framework, unless the community of taggers were a community of literary scholars. Rafferty and Hidderley (2007) identified some of the problems inherent in tagging practice undertaken on Flickr, including the use of tags that are too broad, too specific, 'false' use of terms, private use of language, ambiguity and uncontrolled synonyms. Despite rhetoric that often celebrates the freedom of user-based tagging, there are hints in the literature of the need for post-hoc disciplining of tagging of some sort. The suggestion in the Flickr paper was that the democratic indexing approach could mediate between totally denotative indexing and user-orientated connotative indexing. The modified Hall framework might offer a similar type of solution; that it might provide a structure that could be used to discipline user-based tagging while still allowing for user interpretation and the recording of historical shifts in our understanding of generic history. The fiction retrieval frameworks described in this chapter are theoretical, and clearly pilot-stage ideas at present, but it is hoped that by their inclusion in this book others may be encouraged to further extend research possibilities in this interesting, challenging and highly popular information domain. In particular, and in relation to the pilot studies described in this chapter, possible solutions could be found in using some form of democratic indexing with controlled vocabularies.

References

Barr, A. and Sturges, P. (1992) 'The Fiction Nuisance' in Nineteenth-century Public Libraries, *Journal of Librarianship and Information Science*, **24** (1), 23–32.

Beghtol, C. (1989) Access to Fiction: a problem in classification theory and practice, Part 1, *International Classification*, **16** (3), 134–40.

Beghtol, C. (1990) Access to Fiction: a problem in classification theory and practice, Part II, *International Classification* **17** (4), 21–27.

Beghtol, C. (1994) *The Classification of Fiction: the development of a system based on theoretical principles*, Scarecrow Press.

Beghtol, C. (1995) Domain Analysis, Literary Warrant, and Consensus: the case of fiction studies, *JASIS*, **46** (1), 30-44

Buchanan, G. et al. (2005) Information Seeking by Humanities Scholars, *Lecture Notes in Computer Science*, **3652**, 218–29.

Dowd, G., Stevenson, L. and Strong, J. (eds) (2006) *Genre Matters: essays in theory and criticism*, Intellect.

Eagleton, T. (1996) *Literary Theory: an introduction*, Blackwells.

Ekvall, I.-L. and Larsson, S. (1997) EDVIN – A Search System for Fiction Based on the Experience of Users' Needs, *Information Services and Use*, **17**, 81–4.

Fowler, A. (1982) *Kinds of Literature: an introduction to the theory of genres and modes*, Clarendon.

Frow, J. (2006) *Genre*, Routledge.

Hall, S. (2001) Encoding/decoding. In McKenna, M. G. and Kellner, D. M. (eds), *Media and Cultural Studies: keyworks*, Blackwells, 166–77.

Hidderley, R. and Rafferty, P. (1997) Democratic Indexing: an approach to the retrieval of fiction, Information Services and Use, **17** (2–3), 101–11.

Hubler, E. (1987) *A Note on the Sources of 'Hamlet'*, in *Shakespeare's Hamlet*, Signet.

Immroth, J.P. (1974) Information Needs for the Humanities. In Debons, A., *Information Science: search for identity: proceedings of the 1972 Nato Advanced Study Institute of Information Science*, Dekker, 249–62.

Kristeva, J. (1986 [1966]) Word, Dialogue, and the Novel. In Moi, T. (ed.), *The Kristeva Reader*, Columbia University Press, 35–61.

Pejtersen, A. M. (1978) Fiction and Library Classification, *Scandinavian Public Library Quarterly*, **11** (1), 5–12.

Pejtersen, A. M. (1979) The Meaning of 'About' in Fiction Indexing and Retrieval, *Aslib Proceedings*, **31** (5), 251–7.

Pejtersen, A. M. (1989) The 'Bookhouse': an icon based database system for fiction retrieval in public libraries. In Clausen, H. (ed.), *Information and Innovation: proceedings of the seventh Nordic conference for information and documentation. Arhus, Denmark: Arhus University*, 165–78.

Pejtersen, A. M. (1994) A Framework for Indexing and Representation of Information Based on Work Domain Analysis: a fiction classification analysis. In *Knowledge Organization and Quality Management: proceedings of the Third International ISKO Conference, Copenhagen, Denmark, 20–24 June 1994*, Indeks Verlag, 251–63.

Pejtersen, A. M. and Austin, J. (1983) Fiction Retrieval: experimental design and evaluation of a search system based on users' value criteria (part 1), *Journal of Documentation*, **39** (4), 230–46.

Pejtersen, A. M. and Austin, J. (1984) Fiction Retrieval: experimental design and evaluation of a search system based on users' value criteria (part 2), *Journal of Documentation*, **40** (1), 25–35.

Plassard, M. (ed.) (1998) *IFLANET Functional Requirements for Bibliographic Records: final report*, UBCIM Publications New Series, Vol. 19, K. G. Saur, www.ifla.org/vii/s13/frbr/frbr.htm.

Rafferty, P. (2008) Identifying Diachronic Transformations in Popular Culture Genres: a cultural-materialist approach to the history of popular literature publishing, *Library History*, **24** (4), 262–72.

Rafferty, P. (2009) Replicate, Modify, Challenge: the relationships between author-as-consumer and author-as-producer in popular culture genres, *International Journal of the Book*, **6** (2), 77–84.

Rafferty, P. (2010) Genre Theory, Knowledge Organisation and Fiction. In Gnoli, C. and Mazzocchi, F. (eds), *Paradigms and Conceptual Systems in Knowledge Organization: proceedings of the Eleventh International ISKO Conference (Rome, Italy, 23–26 February 2010)*, Advances in Knowledge Organization, no. 12, Ergon, 254–61.

Rafferty, P. and Hidderley, R. (2005) *Indexing Multimedia and Creative Works: the problem of meaning and interpretation*, Ashgate.

Rafferty, P. and Hidderley, R. (2007) Flickr and Democratic Indexing: dialogic approaches to indexing, *Aslib Proceedings*, **59** (4/5), 397–410.

Ranta, J. A. (1991) The New Literary Scholarship and a Basis for Increased Subject Catalog Access to Imaginative Literature, *Cataloging and Classification Quarterly*, **14** (1), 3–27.

Riesthuis, G. J. A. (1997) Fiction in Need of Transcending Traditional Classification,

Information Services and Use, **17** (2/3), 133–8.

Rowley, J. and Farrow, J. (2000) *Organizing Knowledge: an introduction to managing access to information,* Gower.

Saarti, J. (1999) Fiction Indexing and the Development of Fiction Thesauri, *Journal of Librarianship and Information Science,* **31** (2), 85–92.

Saarti, J. (2000) Taxonomy of Novel Abstracts Based on Empirical Findings, *Knowledge Organization,* **27** (4), 213-20.

Saarti, J. (2002) Fiction Indexing by Library Professionals and Users, *Scandinavian Public Library Quarterly,* **33** (4), 6–9.

Sapp, G. (1986) The Levels of Access: subject approaches to fiction, *RQ,* **25** (4), 488–97.

Vernitski, A. (2007) Developing an Intertextuality-oriented Fiction Classification, *Journal of Librarianship and Information Science,* **39** (1), 41–52.

Walker, R. S. (1970) The Library and the Novel: the treatment of the novel in the libraries: proposals for its fuller exploitation and an outline of a new scheme of classification, University of Strathclyde.

Warner, J. (2010) *Human Information Retrieval,* MIT Press.

Whichbook.com, www.whichbook.net/.

4

Music information retrieval research

Charlie Inskip

Introduction

There is a long history of music librarianship in the domain of printed Western classical music. Special schemes have been developed to aid in the organization and retrieval of musical works, and existing schemes have been widely used to include these types of documents in larger physical library collections. However, the advent of digital consumer technology in the form of MP3 players and mobile phones, combined with the enormous impact of the internet and the digitization and ease of compression of audio files, has brought new formats and types of user interaction to the fore. This has led to an explosion in music information-retrieval research, concentrating on how most beneficially to use computers to organize, search and retrieve music information and recordings from large digital collections.

Many of us today carry around music collections of thousands of digitized music recordings and access all manner of types of music on the web, but still are unsure what to listen to next: the enormous size of these collections and the instant accessibility of 8 million Western pop, classical, jazz and folk songs can cause confusion and trepidation. Where the classical music researcher would previously have consulted academic texts and visited a specialist music library, or the post-rock listener would have read the *New Musical Express* and visited the Rough Trade shop for advice on what was coming up, now we access music through hand-held devices and laptops. The issue is no longer 'I hope I can find that Velvet Underground live album somewhere this year, I wonder what it sounds like', but 'Which Velvet Underground live track shall I read about/ download/stream now?'

Efficient and effective automated retrieval tools can help users to access globally distributed and personal digital music libraries. Recent research in this area generally involves extracting musical features from audio files and using these features to make comparisons between pieces of music in order to determine whether or not they are similar. Enormous data resources from internet usage and unfeasibly large music collections are used for machine learning to enable auto-tagging. The web is trawled for socio-cultural information, and algorithms are developed and tested by a thriving scientific community. Although some of this work is hampered by the fear of breaking copyright regulations, great steps are being made to allow users to engage more actively with digital music recordings in almost utopian ways.

This chapter examines how the special nature of music impacts on the retrieval of digital audio and provides a critical overview of developments in the area of music information retrieval. Important musical facets are introduced and discussed in relation to the communication of musical meaning. This discussion leads to an analysis of various metadata schemas. Prevalent retrieval tools and systems are examined and key approaches to retrieval are identified. The importance of the music user as both a key source of research data and the ultimate participant of the musical communication process is discussed and existing approaches to the evaluation of music retrieval tools and systems are presented and considered.

What is music information?

The very term 'music information retrieval' (MIR) suggests that there is information within music that can be used for retrieval purposes: a user may wish to retrieve a particular piece of music information ('Find me all the appearances in this song of a G7 chord/sad refrain/lyric to do with excitement') or to retrieve music containing that information ('Find me all the songs with a G7 etc.'). The multi-faceted nature of music includes pitch, tempo, harmony, timbre, editorial, textual and bibliographic facets (Downie, 2003a). Music's lack of the word elements found in text causes problems in identifying 'units of meaning' (Byrd and Crawford, 2002). Looking closely at this idea should help to shed some light on the aims and approaches of MIR research and highlight any areas where this could be improved in some way. Along with 'information' comes 'communication'. Indeed, successful communication relies on information getting from one place to another without too much interference. Identifying how musical meaning is conveyed or transmitted from the composer or performer to the listener should help to determine what it is about music that we need to access in order to enable successful retrieval techniques. A range of communication models of increasing sophistication have been devised to interpret this process (including Shannon and Weaver, 1949; Hall, 1980; Tagg, 1999; Inskip, Macfarlane and Rafferty, 2008). These models generally include:

a sender, a channel, a receiver, a relationship between sender and receiver, an effect, a context in which communication occurs and a range of things to which messages refer.   (McQuail and Windahl, 1993, 5)

Successful communication relies on these elements all working together with minimal interference.

As the saying goes, 'music is organized sound'. However, this definition could also apply to speech. We need to examine organized sound more deeply if we are to determine fruitful paths to follow that will lead to successful retrieval approaches. The ethnomusicologist Bruno Nettl (2006) writes that music is an art made by combining sounds, a set of physiological processes and a form of communication. Blacking (1973) states that listeners who share cultural experiences are likely to demonstrate similar responses to music and that if the listener shares the experiences of the composer/performer, then musical meaning is more likely to be communicated. This will be affected by socio-cultural contexts. In fact, with no listener and no cultural context notes are just a jumble of noise and music does not exist. In other words, it's not just the notes that matter. Cultural criteria also impact on successful musical communication.

This double-headed aspect, the content and context of music, is central to its understanding. Although it may seem common sense that without the notes there is no music, it is not so obvious that without listeners, and their attendant cognitive and socio-cultural mechanisms, music does not exist. If music can happen only by being listened to, then it necessarily follows that humans are as important in the process of musical communication as the notes themselves.

Music has a number of facets. These facets vary within and between pieces, contributing towards their identifiability and uniqueness. A song may have been performed many times by one performer. Recordings of these performances are likely to vary. Recordings of classical works, which are generally interpreted within a relatively strict framework expressed by notation and historical tradition, may vary only minutely. Recordings of performances of his own material by Bob Dylan may be almost unrecognizable from one recording to another. Identifying a song, therefore, relies on the listener's knowing something about its content. This can be broken down into key facets at varying levels of complexity. Different sounds can be identified by their pitch (how high or low they are), their intensity (their loudness) and their timbre (the variation between sounds with the same pitch and intensity from two different sources). However pitch, intensity and timbre do not make music (although perhaps some Futurists and Avant Noise aficionados may disagree).

To become music, a collection of sounds has to be organized musically: some may have a beat (tempo), tonality (an agreed relationship between the notes) is likely to be important, a time signature and a key signature may indicate some structure and, possibly, lyrics and a title may be used to connect the sounds in a coherent way. Music has both horizontal nature, unfolding through time, and a vertical nature, expressed by the relationship between its notes. Notes have different onsets – a drum attacks a note while a violin may fade in. They have different lengths and different endings. This multitude of musical elements – and this list does not attempt to be comprehensive – illustrates the special nature of music and gives some indication of the problems inherent in its organization. Combine this multi-faceted nature with a plethora of representations – including written notation, MIDI (Musical Instrument Digital Interface) guitar tabs and audio containers ranging from wax cylinders to mobile phones, and the information management and retrieval challenges presented by music are enormous.

The way in which we engage with music also highlights some key attributes that are negotiated and agreed by society. After the important bibliographic categories of artist, title, composer, work etc., the overarching genres of art (or classical), pop and folk have enormous influence on music organization. Art music requires training in order to appreciate it and has a known composer; folk music has no known composer and evolves through use in the community; and pop music is defined by the relationship between performer and listener and is gauged in terms of commercial success (Brackett, 2000).

These ideas are a step forward from the more traditional definitions of the three musics, which focused on their geographic sources (Redfern, 1978) and reflect the global nature of these genres. Indeed, Brackett's definitions may be applied to music from any culture, and not exclusively to the usual focus on Western music. However, once these three genres are broken down into the more specific hierarchical types enjoyed by record-company marketing campaigns they tend to become more fuzzy as they become more granulated. The difference between pop and rock, dance and R & B, roots and traditional is likely to vary between listeners. Genre can be used as a cultural identifier ('I like punk and garage bands therefore I am a rebellious outsider', 'I enjoy Romanticism but Modernists get my goat') and is traditionally the way to explore CDs in a store. Despite genre's flexible nature causing some problems in organizing materials, it is the predominant category used in many universal digital and physical music collections. Musical context can also be identified by the mood the music attempts to communicate, or the mood it generates in the listener, its novelty, availability or even its use. A tag cloud of musical moods (Figure 4.1, overleaf) illustrates the plethora of emotional attributes that may be applied to music. Finding shared definitions of these can be extremely difficult.

It is occasionally suggested that the subject of lyrics would be a useful access point. This may arise in specialist catalogues designed to find music to accompany moving images, for example; or user-generated tags on social

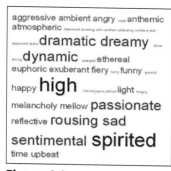

Figure 4.1
Music moods (Inskip, Macfarlane and Rafferty, 2009)

networking sites such as last.FM may refer to 'songs about puppies/existentialism/cities etc.' (last.FM, 2010).

It is the combination of all of these attributes that makes music information retrieval a challenging and exciting area. If we can successfully identify important facets suitable for analysis and categorization, this will take us one step closer to retrieval systems that meet user information needs.

Music and its organization

Historically, in pursuit of successfully organizing large collections of music, general schemes such as Dewey, Library of Congress, Bliss, Brown and Colon all have varying abilities in accommodating the special nature of music. However, these schemes were originally designed for printed texts and do not consider some issues relating particularly to modern popular music, such as multiple authors (composers, performers, producers or remixers), the likelihood of the performer's also being the author, the extraordinary range of genres and the difficulty in identifying music's subject. Eric Coates's specialist scheme, British Catalogue of Music (BCM), is based on Ranganathan's Colon classification. It was the dominant notated Western classical music classification scheme in music libraries from 1957, but its focus on printed literature and printed scores has meant that it has limited application for recorded music.

As large digital collections are so widespread and tend to serve different user bases it has been suggested by the International Association of Sound and Audiovisual Archives (IASA) (Bradley, 2009) that it is not relevant to call for a 'discographic' metadata standard, but rather to adopt metadata infrastructures that are versatile, extensible and sustainable, with modularity, granularity, liquidity, openness and transparency and that are relational (2009, 15). It suggests that schemes should be informed by the key categories of descriptive (content, artist, title, composer, performer), structural (CD number, track number) and administrative metadata (format, barcode, catalogue number). Applying the principles of Functional Requirements of Bibliographic Records (FRBR, 1997) (Work, expression, manifestation, item; Person, corporate body; Concept, object, event, place) to any such scheme should ensure that it will be sufficiently comprehensive to meet a wide range of user information needs, and this approach is flexible enough to reflect the varying requirements of different collections.

This lack of existing standards has led to a proliferation of schemes in music organization, including ID3 tags, MPEG-7, Music XML, Music Ontology, Music

Vocabulary, free DB and MusicBrainz. An analysis of the metadata fields offered by these schemes (Corthaut et al., 2008) concurred with IASA, recommending that the scheme used should be the one that meets users' information needs. Some of these schemes, notably MPEG-7 (MPEG-7, 2004) and Music Ontology (Music Ontology, 2010), are extremely comprehensive, attempting to incorporate all relevant musical concepts, while others (those employed by freeDB [freeDB, 2010] and MusicBrainz [MusicBrainz, 2010], for example) are more focused on consumer-users and do not include extensive amounts of technical administrative information.

Perhaps one of the currently most widely used schemes is ID3v2 tags, used in conjunction with MP3 files (Nilsson, 2000). More than 70 fields can be completed in cataloguing a piece of music using these tags, which follow the 'descriptive, structural, administrative' and FRBR principles, including Album/Movie/Show title, Composer, Media type, Publisher, Artist/Performer etc. (Nilsson, 2000). This approach informs the metadata employed by iTunes, the world's premier legitimate deliverer of downloadable audio and is, perforce, adopted by consumer-users of these products. These editable fields are populated manually by rights holders and thence automatically by commercial database services such as Gracenote (Gracenote, 2010) when CDs are copied to libraries using iTunes software. Users have administrative editing access once the files have been ingested into their hard drives.

While ID3 and other schemes lean towards identifying the bibliographic elements of music, predominantly from an administrative slant, there are also instances of schemes that approach music from another angle. The Pandora 'Music Genome Project' (Pandora, 2010) reportedly considers such musical content features as Instrumentation, Feel, Structures and Influences in its cataloguing. This content-based focus is designed to allow Pandora's internet-radio service to make song recommendations to listeners based on their listening behaviour. A seed song or artist is chosen by the user and tracks with matching facets are presented on the user interface on a player. This approach to music similarity attempts to incorporate some contextual elements as well as musical content and has proved to be very successful in the US marketplace. Similar services such as last.FM are informed by user behaviour, but instead of the expert cataloguers employed by Pandora rely on playcounts and user-generated tags to make their recommendations.

In terms of comprehension, the Music Ontology, developed using RDF/XML, uses three levels of 'expressiveness': editorial information, music creation information and even decomposition (Music Ontology, 2010). The use of Resource Description Framework (RDF) allows Music Ontology to bring in other ontologies that may be required. This means that a range of pre-existing vocabularies may be combined to reflect the complex nature of music and recognizes the impossibility of making an all-encompassing music ontology without access to existing ideas that are so freely available on the semantic web, including friend of a friend (FOAF), FRBR and others. A close look at the terms used in this approach reveals the highly bibliographic nature of this ontology. Combining Classes, Properties and Individuals is indeed comprehensive and, because it is based on identifiable and widely agreed and confirmable facets, allows users access to a large selection of content and contextual information drawn from the semantic web.

Specialist schemes have also been employed in music industry business-to-business services to aid the exploitation of recordings and compositions. The use of music in films, for example, requires catalogues to be searchable not by artist and title but by subject, tempo and mood. One of the earlier schemes is drawn from a collection of mainly classical romantic pieces bound together in a volume and supplied to cinemas for musicians to accompany silent movies. These pieces are organized according to the mood or subject of the action on the screen, including Battle, Birds, Chase, Chatter, Fire-fighting, Grotesque, Humorous, Misterioso, National, Neutral, Orgies, Passion, Pulsating, Purity, Race, Railroad, Sea-storm, Western (Rapee, 1924). Identifying these types of highly subjective facets requires deep insights into the ways potential users think about music, and these contextual ideas are likely to change over time and across cultures.

In summary, although general schemes may be sufficient to incorporate printed notation and music textbooks, a more specialist approach is required to accommodate the complexities of music audio. The enormous variety of music information required according to the nature of the collection and the information needs of the users means that it may be more appropriate to use flexible cataloguing approaches rather than to rely on rigid standards.

MIR systems

The enormous value of digital audio is that the user can access a wide range of material quickly, rather than being reliant on physical collections, which may not be as comprehensive or relevant. Music collections, either held locally on a user's hard drive or remotely accessible via the world wide web, can be accessed by specialist software, which interrogates metadata and presents the user with an organized scheme appropriate to their particular use. A wide range of applications are used by consumers and professionals, including: music library/encyclopedia, personal collection management, commerce and transactions, music editing/production, music playback, music recommend-ation, music retrieval, musical notation (Corthaut et al., 2008). Many of these applications can be served simply by using text retrieval approaches to metadata. Finding a track to download on iTunes or to stream using Spotify or Napster, for example, is a simple process if the listener knows the artist and the title of the track or album they are intending to listen to, while finding information about an artist is relatively intuitive using web services such as All Music Guide. What are of particular interest today, however, are issues surrounding problems such as comprehensive automatic cataloguing (how can a rights holder tag 8 million songs accurately, quickly and cheaply?) and unknown-item search (how can a listener find music they are going to like but haven't heard yet?).

In the late 1990s peer-to-peer networks took immense advantage of the portability of MP3 audio and the interconnectivity of the world wide web. Napster software allowed users to 'share' music on their hard drives with other users. Because of the inherent copyrights of recorded music this prompted a landmark legal case in 2000 which forced Napster to cease operations in that form. Major players in the record industry then gradually agreed with Apple that they should make digital recordings available on the internet for download at a price via the iTunes music store. Other services have since arisen across the internet, mainly serving the sale and distribution of commercial Western popular music and employing schemes focused on bibliographic metadata.

Although the term 'music information retrieval' was first coined in the 1960s by Michael Kassler, who was working on a system to perform Schenkerian analysis on classical notated music (Kassler, 1966), it was not until the Napster case was at the forefront of the media in 2000 that the first International Symposium on Music Information Retrieval (ISMIR) was convened in Plymouth, MA, USA (Downie, Byrd and Crawford, 2009). The event, which since then has taken place annually in various locations around the world, is the primary focus for academics working on music information-retrieval issues and has been extremely influential in providing a serious academic forum in this area. ISMIR encourages a multi-disciplinary approach to MIR research and aims to attract academics and professionals from the areas of computer science, library and information management, musicology, psychology and sociology, as well as musicians and other types of users. The main strand of interest is in the development of computer-based tools such as algorithms to determine various aspects of music that may be used in systems that are designed to enhance user engagement with digital audio. Key areas of research include content-based querying, classification (particularly by genre, style and mood), recommendation and playlist generation, fingerprinting and digital rights management, score following and audio alignment, transcription and annotation, tempo induction and beat tracking, summarization, streaming, text and web mining, optical music recognition, and database systems and indexing and query languages (Dixon, 2008). The tools under investigation are tested by their developers and then submitted to a formal evaluation process, known as MIREX, the results of which are presented at each annual conference. These evaluations are discussed later on in this chapter.

The work of ISMIR is so wide ranging and fast moving that it would be a disservice to attempt to summarize it. Some important themes have arisen throughout the ten years of the conference that are particularly relevant to the field of information retrieval.

Musical relevance

Information retrieval is concerned with the searching of large (text) collections, normally evaluated by relevance, which is evaluated by precision and recall. These measures rely on an agreed ground truth – a document is either relevant or not relevant. Experimental relevance of text documents is generally determined by whether or not they meet the needs of the user or solve the user's anomalous state of knowledge (Belkin, Oddy and Brooks, 1982). In MIR this approach presents some difficulties.

Firstly, the concept of relevance is not as clear cut in music as it may be in text. Although in known-item searching it is easy to present the 'right' result from a search using artist and title, once the facets such as genre, subject, mood and similarity are driving a query, then relevance becomes much more difficult to pin down. Precision and recall are equally difficult to determine with these subjective facets. These difficulties become paramount in the annual MIREX evaluations, where it is unusual for precision and recall to be used to evaluate tools under submission, and 'accuracy' and a range of statistical measures are brought in.

Musical focus

Much of the research into MIR to date has been undertaken in Western universities, predominantly in the USA and Europe, although more recently in Japan and China, by PhD students in their 20s and 30s. It should not come as too much of a surprise, therefore, to find that the focus in such research is on recorded Western popular music and, to a lesser degree, on notated Western classical music. Although some work has been performed on music from other cultures and Western folk music, these are far outweighed by more popular consumer and educational genres. Jazz is rarely mentioned. This reflects the culture of the community and is similar to the situation in text retrieval, which has tended to concentrate on English-language texts.

The impact of social media

Over the last ten years much work has been done on extracting musical features such as tempo, rhythm, timbre, melody and using these features to make decisions about music recordings in terms of their similarity to others. It is generally assumed that recordings with the same features as others will be deemed to be similar by listeners. It has been found with this content-based approach that there are glass ceilings in terms of accuracy. More recently, researchers have been given access to large amounts of user-generated data, most particularly tags, and are now including these data in their approaches (Barrington, Oda and Lanckriet, 2009). Combining this more contextual approach with content-based algorithms has led to a noticeable improvement in evaluation results. Partly tagged collections are being used in machine learning in order to develop 'auto-tagging' systems (Mandel, Eck and Bengio, 2010; Coviello et al., 2010), and automatic playlist generators based on this combination are becoming more reliable (Barrington, Oda and Lanckriet., 2009).

It was only fair that in the early years of the discipline the MIR community focused on the essential technical development of specific tools for its work. A lot of work needed to be done to exploit the rapid recent changes in technology and the attendant processing power of computers. The recent ten year anniversary of ISMIR gave the community opportunity to pause and reflect on its progress, and may in the future be seen as the pivotal moment when MIR shifted from primarily focusing on systems to incorporating users into the experience and from focusing on tools to development of human-usable systems (Downie, Byrd and Crawford, 2009).

Without a listener . . .

Listeners, or music users, can be drawn from three main areas of interest: casual or recreational listeners, professional users such as musicians and other people using music, such as DJs, and scholars and theorists. Although they are all engaging with music on some level these users may have different information needs, illustrated by a variety of types of query:

- Find me a song that sounds like this.
- Given that I like these songs, find me more songs that I may enjoy.
- I need to organize my personal collection of digital music (stored in my hard drive, portable device, MP3 player, cell phone . . .)
- Retrieve musical works that have a rhythm (melody, harmony, orchestration) similar to this one.
- I am looking for a suitable soundtrack for . . .

Query examples such as the above tend to relate to searches for unknown items. Users often frame their queries in terms of similarity. This 'query by example' is a suitable way to narrow down large collections of broadly similar items. It removes the problem of using textual metadata, which are likely to either be missing (in terms of not knowing the artist or title) or vague and subjective. It can be a lot easier for someone to say 'I'm looking for a song like this' than 'I like songs that have a slow build in the first 30 seconds, are in 3/4 time, have a sax solo in the middle eight, lyrics about puppies and were recorded in the mid-1980s'. The difficulty in framing music queries verbally and the proliferation of mood, genre and other textual terms combined with the variation of musical knowledge of users does create difficulty in solving unknown-item search requests.

Although it is possibly an unsolvable problem, identifying emotion and mood in music is an important element of MIR. If we return to the definition of music as an art combining sounds, then it is important to understand that music requires a listener, and that although specific motivations to listen to music may be many and varied, music is a social process that appears across history and cultures. As it is the ability of music to carry and enhance emotion and mood that makes it an art form rather than a craft (Bicknell, 2009), musical mood is an important facet. Although this facet is not easily categorized and can vary among listeners, there are some generalizations that are applicable to music, such as major key for happy, minor key for sad, heavy beats for triumphant, soft for relaxed. One useful tool widely used in MIR research to identify mood is the Valence/Arousal model (Figure 4.2), which attempts to model human experience of emotion in a two-dimensional scale (Russell, 1980).

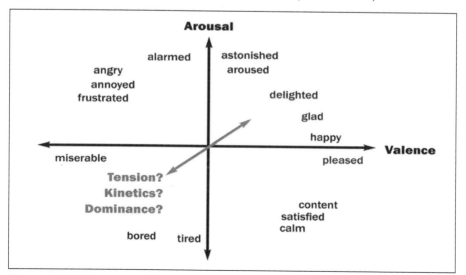

Figure 4.2 *Valence-Arousal space (from Kim et al., 2010)*

Listeners under investigations using this space appear to have similar experiences when listening to music, and mapping their moods as vectors allows them to be manipulated by computers as numerical vectors (Kim et al., 2010). It is vital to involve listeners in mood research: matching musical and contextual features to qualities such as delight, happiness, boredom and frustration requires substantive input from research into human cognitive behaviour. The need for a multi-disciplinary approach to MIR research is freely and regularly acknowledged by the community. The problems of collecting large amounts of reliable data and the need for a 'ground truth' for robust evaluation are being met not only by interviews and focus groups but also creatively by the community, accessing large datasets from last.FM's API and the design of web-based games that collect data from participants listening to music and tagging tracks (Law et al., 2009).

The human side of music listening does not necessarily only involve extremely personal experiences. Many listeners attempt to communicate their interest in music by using the world wide web on social networking sites such as MySpace, last.FM, YouTube and Facebook. This proliferation of human-generated data has been of great value in MIR research. Users seem happy to publish their listening habits and personal music categorizations (as tags) either online through last.FM or via proprietary download services such as iTunes' Genius application. This habitual sharing of data has been widely accessed by researchers and marketers attempting to gain deeper insights into human musical behaviour, and the uptake of playlists generated by these systems is starting to influence listening behaviour (Barrington, Oda and Lanckriet, 2009).

Taking a holistic view (Ingwersen and Järvelin, 2005) of information retrieval systems, these should include not only the tools and machines holding and searching the documents but also the humans using them to satisfy their information needs. Gathering data from listeners is therefore integral to MIR research. This view is supported by the recent development of, in particular, auto-tagging and automatic playlisting systems by the MIR community, which combine elements of both the content and context of music in order to satisfy human listening needs.

Evaluation

The MIR community's evaluation, known as Music Information Retrieval Evaluation eXchange (MIREX), of the tools in development has been informed by a close study of the text retrieval evaluation approaches of TREC (Text REtrieval Conference). The recommendations of a detailed TREC consultation in 2003 focus on three main issues. At the time there were:

1. no standard collection of music against which each team could test its techniques;
2. no standardized sets of performance tasks; and, 3. no standardized evaluation
metrics.
(Downie, 2003b)

The MIREX team has since been continuously developing a robust evaluation
framework for MIR tools. It has collected a large amount of recordings (unique
pieces of music that have been used in evaluations: 143,817; individual audio
files: 228,480) of music drawn from a wide range of styles and genres. To
accommodate intellectual copyright regulations, which prevent MIREX from
supplying these recordings to developers as test-beds, these are held in one
place, accessible only to the MIREX team. Algorithms are submitted annually
by researchers for competition after being tested on the researchers' test
collections. A number of tasks have been devised, changing each year according
to interest from the community. These tasks most recently included: music
similarity (audio and symbolic), audio cover-song identification, auto-tag
classification, query by tapping, humming and singing, and audio tempo
estimation. Algorithms designed to satisfy these tasks are applied to collections
by the MIREX team and ranked results are published at ISMIR.

As the tasks vary conceptually, so their evaluation cannot be standardized. It
is not possible or indeed suitable to evaluate them all using text retrieval's
precision and recall. The main evaluation metric in 2004 and 2005 was accuracy.
Through encouragement from the organizers, precision and recall were more
widely used thereafter, alongside other statistical measures such as p-score, f-
measure, ANOVA (Downie, 2008). It is only through a satisfactory definition of
musical relevance that precision and recall may be more widely used. This is
partly resolved by Downie's suggestion that:

> there should be enough information contained within the query records that
> reasonable persons would concur as to whether or not a given returned item
> satisfied the intention of the query.
> (Downie, 2003c)

As the MIREX evaluations move forward the organizers and the participants
become more experienced and continually learn from previous years of
competition. Human volunteers are recruited from the community to generate
ground-truth data and, most recently, larger numbers of anonymous
participants have been involved through web-based services such as Amazon
Mechanical Turk (Amazon Web Services, 2010). Although this commitment to
gathering human experience of music can be expensive, takes time and is not
always accurate (Downie, 2008), it shows a strong commitment to reliable
evaluation in the discipline, acknowledging the vital involvement of the listener
in successful musical communication.

Conclusion

Although music is sometimes called a language and can communicate certain ideas to the listener, it has many facets that are dissimilar to those of text. These facets are not only found within the music itself, in the form of melody, harmony, tempo and timbre, but are interpreted by the cognitive processes of the listener within frameworks of culturally agreed rules such as genre, style and mood. The last ten years have seen rapid development in the portability and availability of recorded music, leading to a valuable opportunity to engage computer processing power to search through millions of songs to find the ones we wish to listen to, for whatever reason. There is acknowledgement within the MIR community that applying theories and standards developed through the lengthy history of text information retrieval and music librarianship should inform a professional and rigorously academic music-information retrieval research discipline. However there are some issues, such as relevance and a lack of ground truth, that mean new and creative approaches are required in the development of suitable evaluations of tools and systems. If the next ten years of MIR are to see the widespread adoption of systems that use the tools currently being developed by the community, then the continuation of a multi-disciplinary approach and a holistic view of music retrieval will be key to this success.

References

Amazon Web Services (2010) *Amazon Mechanical Turk (beta),* http://aws.amazon.com/mturk.

Barrington, L., Oda, R. and Lanckriet, G. (2009) Smarter than Genius? Human evaluation of music recommender systems. In *Proceedings of International Conference for Music Information Retrieval, Kobe, Japan, 26–30 October, 2009.*

Belkin, N., Oddy, R. and Brooks, H. (1982) ASK for Information Retrieval, *Journal of Documentation,* **38**, 61–71 (part 1) and 145–64 (part 2).

Bicknell, J. (2009) *Why Music Moves Us,* Palgrave Macmillan.

Blacking, J. (1973) *How Musical is Man?* University of Washington Press.

Brackett, D. (2000) *Interpreting Popular Music,* University of California Press.

Bradley, K. (ed.) (2009) *IASA TC-04 Guidelines on the Production and Preservation of Digital Audio Objects,* 2nd edn, International Association of Sound and Audiovisual Archives.

Byrd, D. and Crawford, T. (2002) Problems of Music Information Retrieval in the Real World, *Information Processing and Management,* **38** (2), 249–72.

Corthaut, N., Govaerts, S., Verbert, K. and Duval, E. (2008) Connecting the Dots: music metadata generation, schemas and applications. In *Proceedings of International Conference for Music Information Retrieval, Philadelphia, 14–18 September 2008.*

Coviello, E., Barrington, L., Chan, A. and Lanckriet, G. (2010) Automatic Music Tagging with Time Series Models. *Proceedings of International Conference for Music Information Retrieval, Utrecht, Netherlands, 9–13 August 2010.*

Dixon, S. (2008) Correspondence to Music-IR e-mail list, December.

Downie, J. S. (2003a) Music Information Retrieval. In Cronin, B. (ed.), *Annual Review of Information Science and Technology 37*, Information Today, 295–340.

Downie, J. S. (2003b) Interim Report on Establishing MIR/MDL Evaluation Frameworks: commentary on consensus building, *The MIR/MDL Evaluation Project White Paper Collection Edition #3* (2003), 43–4, www.music-ir.org/evaluation/wp.html.

Downie, J. S. (2003c) Toward the Scientific Evaluation of Music Information Retrieval Systems, *Proceedings of International Symposium on Music Information Retrieval, Baltimore, USA, 27–30 October 2003.*

Downie, J. S. (2008) The Music Information Retrieval Exchange (2005–2007): a window into music information retrieval research, *Acoustic Science and Technology*, **29** (4), 247–55.

Downie, J. S., Byrd, D. and Crawford, T. (2009) Ten Years of ISMIR: reflections on challenges and opportunities, *Proceedings of International Conference for Music Information Retrieval, Kobe, Japan, 26–30 October 2009.*

FRBR (1997) *IFLA*, www.ifla.org/VII/s13/frbr/frbr.pdf.

freeDB (2010) freeDB.org, www.freedb.org/en/.

Gracenote (2010) *Apple iTunes and Genius*, www.gracenote.com/casestudies/itunes/.

Hall, S. (1980) Encoding/Decoding. In Hall, S., Hobson, D., Lowe, A. and Willis, P. (eds), *Culture, Media, Language*, Hutchinson, 128–38.

Ingwersen, P. and Järvelin, K. (2005) *The Turn*, Springer.

Inskip, C., Macfarlane, A. and Rafferty, P. (2008) Meaning, Communication, Music: towards a revised communication model, *Journal of Documentation*, **64** (5) 687–706.

Inskip, C., Macfarlane, A. and Rafferty, P. (2009) Organizing Music for Movies. In *Proceedings of International Society for Knowledge Organization (UK) Content Architecture conference, London, UK, 22–23 June 2009.*

Kassler, M. (1966) Towards Musical Information Retrieval, *Perspectives of New Music*, **4**, 59–67.

Kim, Y., Schmidt, E., Migneco, R., Morton, B., Richardson, P., Scott, J., Speck, J. and Turnbull, D. (2010) Music Emotion Recognition: a state of the art review. In *Proceedings of International Conference for Music Information Retrieval, Utrecht, Netherlands, 9–13 August 2010.*

last.FM (2010) Tag Results for 'Songs About Something', www.last.fm/search?q=songs+about+something&type=tag.

Law, E., West, K., Mandel, M., Bay, M. and Downie, J. S. (2009) Evaluation of Algorithms Using Games: the case of music tagging. In *Proceedings of International Conference for Music Information Retrieval, Kobe, Japan, 26–30 October 2009.*

Mandel, M., Eck, D. and Bengio, Y. (2010) Learning Tags that Vary within a Song. In *Proceedings of International Conference for Music Information Retrieval, Utrecht, Netherlands, 9–13 August 2010*.

McQuail, D. and Windahl, S. (1993) *Communication Models for the Study of Mass Communication*, Longmans.

MPEG-7 (2004) *MPEG-7 Overview*, http://mpeg.chiariglione.org/standards/mpeg-7/mpeg-7.htm.

Music Ontology (2010) *Music Ontology Specification*, http://musicontology.com/.

MusicBrainz (2010) *Welcome to MusicBrainz*, http://musicbrainz.org/.

Nettl, B. (2006) Music. In Macy, L. (ed.), *Grove Music Online*, www.grovemusic.com.

Nilsson, M. (2000) *ID3 tag version 2. – Frames*, www.id3.org/Frames.

Pandora (2010) *The Music Genome Project*, www.pandora.com/mgp.shtml.

Rapee, E. (1974 [1924]) *Motion Picture Moods for Pianists and Organists*, Arno Press.

Redfern, B. (1978) *Organising Music in Libraries, Vol. 1, Arrangement and Classification*, Clive Bingley.

Russell, J. (1980) A Circumplex Model of Affect, *Journal of Personality and Social Psychology*, **39** (6), 1161–78.

Shannon, C. and Weaver, W. (1949) *The Mathematical Theory of Communication*, University of Illinois Press.

Tagg, P. (1999) *Introductory Notes to the Semiotics of Music*, version 3, unpublished, www.tagg.org/xpdfs/semiotug.pdf.

5

—•●•—

Folksonomies, social tagging and information retrieval

Isabella Peters

Introduction

Services in Web 2.0 generate a large quantity of information, distributed over a range of resources (e.g. photos, URLs, videos) and integrated into different platforms (e.g. social bookmarking systems, sharing platforms (Peters, 2009). To adequately use this mass of information and to extract it from the platforms, users must be equipped with suitable tools and knowledge. After all, the best information is useless if users cannot find it: 'The model of information consumption relies on the information being found' (Vander Wal, 2004). In Web 2.0, the retrieval component has been established through so-called folksonomies (Vander Wal, 2005a), which are considered as several combinations of an information resource, one or more freely chosen keywords ('tags') and a user. Web 2.0 services that use folksonomies as an indexing and retrieval tool are defined as 'collaborative information services' because they allow for the collaborative creation of a public database that is accessible to all users (registered, where necessary) via the tags of the folksonomy (Ding et al., 2009; Heymann, Paepcke and Garcia-Molina, 2010).

Folksonomies in information retrieval serve mainly to provide access to information resources for all users – where the initial motivation for tagging is often of a personal nature:

> In my mind, at least initially, it really has do with retaining information that you, I, or anyone else has found and organizing it in a way so that people can re-find that information at some later date. Tagging bookmarks is really another way of trying to keep source [. . .] once found on the Internet permanently found.
>
> (Gordon-Murnane, 2006, 28)

Metadata in the form of tags, titles or descriptions are especially invaluable for the retrieval of non-textual information resources such as images or videos because the state of the art of search engine technology allows only for textual research, meaning that these resources would otherwise be irretrievable (Dye, 2006). In these instances, it is also important for the retrievability of resources to be guaranteed by a broad-access vocabulary, and this is where folksonomy can provide excellent service (Goodrum and Spink, 2001, 296). Because of their strong user-orientedness and broad-access vocabulary, folksonomies can also facilitate the retrieval of relevant information in company intranets or in 'enterprise search' (Schillerwein, 2008).

Nevertheless, even information retrieval with folksonomies must focus on finding relevant resources and avoiding 'ballast', through the use of computer-guided tools (Shardanand and Maes, 1995). It is evident that searching in collaborative information services or, more broadly speaking, in Web 2.0, gives rise to other priorities, which require an adjustment of traditional search options. These priorities can be described by the phrase 'social searching' (Brusilovsky, 2008; Evans and Chi, 2008). Since the term is so broad, it can encompass pretty well all retrieval options that folksonomies support. Smith et al. (2008) formulate six requirements that information retrieval within Web 2.0 and via folksonomies must meet:

1   *Filter*: The user's social context, search, clicking and buying histories (SCSCB) have to be exploited for the compilation of hit lists.
2   *Rank*: SCSCB should also be exploited for the ranking of search results. Furthermore, the popularity and credibility of individual users can be used to balance the ranking.
3   *Disambiguate*: SCSCB can be applied to the adjustment of search results and thus provide relevant results.
4   *Share*: The user's self-produced and self-published content can be exploited in searches.
5   *Recommend*: SCSCB and users' content can be used to recommend products, friends, information etc. without the user having to actively search for it.
6   *Match make*: The recommendation and finding of similar users serves to make business contacts and communicate with team members, experts in certain areas etc. and should not be neglected.

This chapter investigates in how far folksonomies meet the above demands of 'social searching'. In order to stress the necessity of indexing measures for information retrieval, one section focuses on the relationship between information retrieval and knowledge representation (Peters and Stock, 2010). Since the topic of 'information retrieval' encompasses the searching and finding of information in a very general way, and since there are many search paths to finding information (e.g. searching, browsing, retrieving, recommender systems or tag clouds), the chapter will address these first and then discuss the importance of relevance ranking in folksonomy-based systems. Building on this, attention is drawn to the particularities of folksonomies in information retrieval and suggestions are made for further areas of research.

The relation between knowledge representation and information retrieval

The goal and task of information retrieval is to find relevant information within an appropriate time and with an appropriate degree of effort. A truly effective information retrieval system would exploit the groundwork laid by knowledge representation. The task of knowledge representation is to represent the content of an information resource via a vocabulary that is known to both users and indexers (Tudhope and Nielsen, 2006), which is not unproblematic: 'In an information retrieval system, there are at least two, and possibly many more vocabularies present [...] Translating between these vocabularies is often a difficult and defining issue in information systems' (Mathes, 2004).

The alignment of the different vocabularies provides access to the resources and makes information retrieval possible in the first place (Chopin, 2008; Chi and Mytkowicz, 2006). The problem of linguistic variation applies to both areas: in knowledge representation it is concerned with the allocation of adequate concepts and terms; in information retrieval it relates to the finding of adequate search terms, or to knowledge of the indexing terms used. The problem for the user can be summarized as a 'vocabulary problem' (Furnas et al., 1987) or reduced to the simple formula: 'Find what I mean and not what I say!' (Feldman, 2000).

The mass and variety of information resources do not make information retrieval any easier because they result in an equally large variety of terms. Unless a controlled vocabulary is used, neither researcher nor indexer can be aware of the precise terms in advance. However, a controlled vocabulary is often difficult for the average user to learn. Furthermore, such vocabularies often appear constructed and artificial and do not reflect users' normal language (Chen, 1994).

This is where folksonomies enter the fray. Folksonomies can reflect a broad range of linguistic terms and concepts and thus broaden the access paths to information resources. They are capable of bridging the 'semantic gap' between different groups of users and thus enhance the power of information retrieval in a fundamental way (Jörgensen, 2007). Furnas et al. (1987) adopt a quantity-oriented approach and encourage designers of information retrieval systems to allow for as many search terms as possible:

Clearly the only hope for untutored vocabulary driven access is to provide many, many alternate entry terms. [. . .] The proposal here is to allow essentially unlimited numbers of aliases.   (Furnas et al., 1987, 968)

It is important to emphasize that the 'vocabulary problem' is not new, nor did it first emerge with the creation of tagging systems. The problem of the precision of terms has a bearing on any attempt to introduce a meta-level that is intended to represent the objects referred to. Because of their liberal nature, folksonomies are supposed to provide a means of counteracting the problem of the limitations of descriptors and a means of broadening access paths to information resources via collective indexing.

Searching – browsing – retrieving

Users can pursue different paths in order to satisfy an information need. These can be divided into roughly two approaches: the pull approach, and the push approach. Both approaches are implemented within collaborative information services with the help of folksonomies (Begelman, Keller and Smadja, 2006). The pull approach is represented by active searches via tags or by the different visualizations of folksonomies, e.g. tag clouds; the push approach by subscription to RSS feeds (Tredinnick, 2006) on the basis of tags or users. An active search via tags, i.e. entering search tags into a search form, works the same way as in online search engines or library catalogues: the search term is compared to the indexing terms or the terms in the full text and, if there is a match, the resource in question is retrieved as a search result.

Folksonomies make use of the language and views of users and function without a restricted indexing or knowledge organization system (KOS). Thus they can broaden access paths to resources and, in the case of non-textual resources (e.g. images), make them accessible in the first place (Jörgensen, 2007). According to Gruber (2005) and Hammond et al. (2005) their liberal design makes folksonomies a perfect research tool. Gruber writes that '[f]or the task of finding information, taxonomies are too rigid and purely text-based search is too weak' (Gruber, 2005), while Hammond et al. (2005) suggest that:

This provision of rich, structured metadata means that the user is provided with an accurate third-party identification of a document, which could be used to retrieve that document, but is also free to search on user-supplied terms so that documents of interest (or rather, references to documents) can be made discoverable and aggregated with other similar descriptions either recorded by the user or by other users.

Weiss (2005) also regards the collaborative creation of folksonomies, as well as collaborative indexing of information resources, as folksonomies' greatest advantages, particularly for browsing. Crawford (2006) does not rate retrieval via tags quite so highly, and criticizes the very unpredictability of folksonomies, which, in particular, has a bearing on the duration of searches because folksonomies are 'lowering the cost for those who might wish to identify, but increasing the cost (in time) for those searching' (2006). Cox, Clough and Marlow (2008) argue that collaborative information services such as Flickr are not oriented towards intentional search for resources at all, and that tags are not necessary for searching because other textual information (e.g. title, description) is available in abundance. If, on the other hand, tags are regarded as metadata that provide an additional description of the resource's content, thus returning to the basic idea of controlled vocabularies, then folksonomies are actually way ahead of online search engines and full-text searching. Wash and Rader (2006) summarize:

> The average site has only 26% of its tags appearing in the webpage at all. We believe that this is evidence that the tags provide useful metadata that is not directly available in the webpage. [. . .] This allows users to search and filter using words that do not appear in the target document, something normal internet search engines are not very good at.

In tagging systems, the terms 'pivot browsing', which refers to the ability to reorientate browsing to follow tags or users' names, for example (Millen, Feinberg and Kerr, 2006; Sinha, 2006), and 'exploratory search' (Millen, Whittaker and Feinberg, 2007) are repeatedly used to describe information retrieval. The concept of 'serendipity' (Merton, 1949; Mathes, 2004; Auray, 2007; Tonkin et al., 2008) is closely related to the retrieval strategy of browsing.

With folksonomies, pivot browsing can be performed via tags (leading the user to all resources indexed with these tags), persons/users (leading the user to a person's profile as well as to their resources and tags) or resources (leading the user to the resource itself and to the indexed tags and the persons who have also saved the resource) (Hotho et al., 2006a, 2006c; Choy and Lui, 2006). Browsing is mainly supported by the various visualization methods of folksonomies.

In particular, the design of tagging systems, and the representation of folksonomies within them, can influence and, at their best, support browsing. Heymann and Garcia-Molina (2006) discuss the representations of folksonomies prevalent today and their options for starting a search:

1   A list of all objects which are tagged with a given tag (or possibly a combination of two or more tags).

2   A list of the most popular tags in the system.
3   A list of tags which have a high degree of overlap with a tag the user is currently investigating.

Pivot browsing through resources, tags and users leads the user to the desired information. This procedure can be relatively time consuming because, if he is not promptly directed to his goal, the user is continually distracted by new resources or better tags. Direct clicking on tags in a tag cloud must be excluded here, however, since it is not fundamentally different from an active search via tags – in both cases, the user is presented with the resources that have been indexed with the tag in question.

Searching and browsing are different in terms of the amount of cognitive effort required of the user in order to satisfy his information need. Xu et al. (2006) hold that active searches are less demanding:

> Tagging bridges some gap between browsing and search. Browsing enumerates all objects and finds the desirable one by exerting the recognition aspect of the human brain, whereas search uses association and dives directly to the interested objects, and thus is mentally less obnoxious.

The tripartite network of resources, tags and users is the factor that can best be exploited for browsing within collaborative information services. The network's human factor, in particular, seems to make browsing attractive to users. They want to link up with other users, to be a part of the community and to find out what resources their contacts are reading, saving, uploading or rating (Mislove et al., 2008). This phenomenon has a bearing on the description of another variant of browsing: 'social browsing' (Lerman and Jones, 2006) or 'social navigation' (Dieberger, 1997; Svensson, 1998; Dieberger et al., 2000). Here, the user no longer finds his information by actively searching, but through the users in his network:

> Social navigation utilizes the fact that most information navigation in the real world is performed through talking to other people. When we need to find information about an illness, we talk to our relatives, friends and medical doctors ...
> (Forsberg, Höök and Svensson, 1998)

Since the members of a community often share the same interests, a user can assume that resources saved by members he knows will also be interesting to him (Sen et al., 2006). In the most extreme scenario, the user is automatically sent news of his community, so that information retrieval shifts from the pull approach to the push approach. Social navigation depends on users' collaboration and activity, since the behaviour of one user will influence another, thus facilitating the exchange between the two (Freyne and Smyth, 2004; Sandusky, 2006; Freyne et al., 2007; Blank et al., 2008; Brusilovsky, 2008). Social navigation is very close to collaborative filtering. Nevertheless, here, as with active searches, the problem arises of the variability of linguistic terms. The meaning of the tags must be known if one is to profit from social navigation and find relevant resources. Sen et al. (2006, 181) point out this difficulty: 'Social navigation may be more powerful in communities that share a common vocabulary. As an extreme example, people who speak different languages will find little value in each other's tags'.

The problem of linguistic variability also arises again with another way of using tags for retrieval: the finding of resources already known to a user. Studies on users' tagging behaviour (e.g. Brooks and Montanez, 2006a, 2006b; Marlow et al., 2006a, 2006b; Pluzhenskaia, 2006; Xu et al., 2006) show that tags are used mainly for personal resource management. Here, too, there is a danger that users may at some point forget what tags they used with which meaning or for which resource (Muller, 2007). By dealing predominantly with their own resource management and indexing via tags, users of tagging systems serve such systems in two ways: 1) by creating content, and 2) by creating an individual retrieval infrastructure (Dye, 2006). And this infrastructure, initially created for selfish reasons, helps all users in retrieval through its multitude of search entries. This form of collaboration in the creation of a retrieval system is regarded by Dye (2006, 40) as the greatest advantage of folksonomies: 'Collaboration through collective tagging gives members of these communities a chance to build their own search systems from the ground up, based on their own vocabularies, interests, and ideas'.

Folksonomy-based recommender systems

In collaborative information services the user can be presented with recommendations for successful information retrieval in two ways: 1) through collaborative filtering systems, and 2) through tag recommender systems for formulating queries.

Collaborative filtering systems serve as recommender systems for relevant information on the basis of user behaviour, the relations between users of an information platform (Lambiotte and Ausloos, 2006) and the push approach. This type of system exploits the networking function of folksonomies, which connects users with information resources via tags and regards users with similar tastes as 'tag buddies' (Paolillo and Penumarthy, 2007; Fokker, Pouwelse and Buntine, 2006). Users who index, save, edit etc. the same resources are linked bibliographically. In tag recommender systems resources are linked thematically if they have been indexed with the same tags (Figure 5.1).

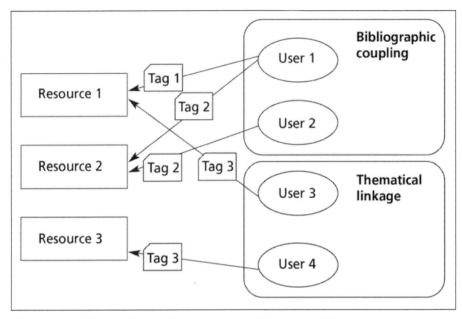

Figure 5.1 *Bibliographic coupling and thematical linkage in folksonomies*

Folksonomy-based filtering or recommender systems are thus generally able to suggest two kinds of information: people or resources (John and Seligmann, 2006). Diederich and Iofciu (2006) summarize the suggestions that can be made on the basis of user profiles and tags:

1   *objects based on users*: recommendation of other resources based on other users
2   *users based on objects*: recommendation of other users based on other resources
3   *users based on co-tagging*: recommendation of other users based on identically/similarly tagged resources
4   *tags based on users*: tag recommendation based on identical/similar users
5   *users based on tags*: recommendation of other users based on identical/similar tags.

Much more important than recommendation of similar resources, though, would seem to be recommendation of similar or relevant users in collaborative information services (Wash and Rader, 2007; Diederich and Iofciu, 2006; Farrell et al., 2007). 'As such, a collaborative tagging system helps users in not only retrieving information but also socializing with others' (Wu, Zubair and Maly, 2006, 112). Users are interested mainly in other users, their resources and their opinions. Panke and Gaiser (2008) interviewed roughly 200 users about their tagging behaviour and found that two-thirds of the interviewees used tags to meet new people. The motto of information gathering is now: 'More like me!' – find users who are similar to me so I can find relevant information by watching them (Smith et al., 2008). It can be assumed that users are similar or have similar interests if they use the same tags (Chopin, 2008), or if they are connected to resources via the same relations, or if they index the same resources.

Diederich and Iofciu (2006) regard a user's tags as his 'interest profile' and then compare users on that basis. Here, two steps must be considered: the first step in recommending users consists in calculating the similarities between the initial user and all other users of the information platform via a coefficient. The calculation must be performed in two stages in order to do justice to the users' thematic linking, on the one hand, and to their bibliographic matching, on the other. Van Damme, Hepp and Siorpaes (2007) arrive at the same conclusion and call this procedure the exploitation of two light-weight ontologies: the 'sub-communities' (bibliographic coupling) and the 'object overlaps' (same tags). With regard to thematic linking, it must be observed for each similarity coefficient (e.g. the cosine) that: a is the number of tags allocated by user 1, b is the number of tags allocated by user i, and g is the number of tags used by both together. For bibliographic coupling: a is the number of resources indexed by user 1, b the number of resources indexed by user i, and g the number of resources indexed by both. The two values calculated can then be summarized and will determine the degree of similarity between two users. Typical approaches for the calculation of similarity that might be used in this first step are Cosine similarity, the Dice coefficient or the Jaccard-Sneath coefficient. The second step (if one follows the more elaborate variant and neglects the k-nearest-neighbours classification procedure, for example) now includes the formation of clusters or communities of users via the Single-Link, Complete-Link or Group-Average-Link clustering procedures. The most-similar users thus determined can then be suggested to user 1.

An elaborate system for discovering similar users and communities via identical tags is introduced by Alani et al. (2003) with 'Ontocopi'. They use the relations of an ontology as tags and thus link resources and users. Another approach for folksonomy-based person recommender systems is presented by John and Seligmann (2006). Here, users of the corporate intranet who use a particular tag very often for describing their saved resources are considered experts for this tag (see also Schillerwein, 2008). Van Damme, Hepp and Siorpaes (2007) discuss the development of recommender systems based on different information platforms in order to increase the range of analysable data. Heck and Peters (2010) developed a system for expert recommendation based on tags, resources and users in scientific social bookmarking systems.

The tripartite relation of tags–users–resources can further be exploited in order to generate automatic suggestions for the expansion of search requests or for indexing on the basis of a tag's, a user's or a resource's placement in the network (Diederich and Iofciu, 2006; Bischoff et al., 2010; Fu et al., 2010; Liu et al., 2009). Recommendations of better or more similar search terms are also presented under the 'query expansion' option (Efthimiadis, 1996; 2000). Recall is enhanced through expansion with related terms, hyperonyms (broader terms), hyponyms (narrower terms) and synonyms (in descending order), while precision is enhanced through query expansion via synonyms, hyponyms, hyperonyms and related terms (in descending order) (Greenberg, 2001, 409). The use of tag recommendations for query expansion and information retrieval is confirmed by Brooks and Montanez (2006a, 2006b). The candidates for tag recommendation and query expansion can be generated in various ways; Stock's (2007a, 486) summary, below, is complemented by points 1 and 6:

1   co-occurrence in a resource
2   co-occurrence in a cluster
3   identical terminology
4   relations, via references or citations
5   neighbourhood in a social network
6   alignment with knowledge organization networks.

Simple recommender systems merely recommend the top *n* tags of the folksonomy's co-occurring tags. An enhancement of this method is the formation of tag clusters via known similarity coefficients and cluster procedures in order to generate semantic webs of the indexed tags and to use these for recommendation (Begelman, Keller, and Smadja, 2006). Grahl, Hotho and Stumme (2007) form clusters from the Delicious folksonomy via the 'KMeans-Cluster' algorithm. Capocci and Caldarelli (2008) work with cluster analysis and use it to check the probability of two hierarchically linked tags being annotated. Brooks and Montanez (2006a) investigate the expressiveness of tags in blog posts, but concentrate on the comparison of user-generated tags and tags automatically extracted from the full texts of blogs. The cluster analysis of both kinds of tags shows that the terms from the tag clusters are less similar to one another than are the terms from tag clusters calculated with TF*IDF (Term Frequency – Inverse Document Frequency weight).

If the recommender system can use full texts or other metadata for its analysis, the comparison of the resource terminology can occur within the search results

(Cui et al., 2002). Thus, first of all similar resources are found and they are then used to extract tag suggestions via TF*IDF. This procedure can also be used to generate tags for previously untagged resources, as Graham, Eoff and Caverlee (2008) find. The system 'AutoTag' (Mishne, 2006) also works according to this principle and recommends tags for blog posts.

Since the tagging of a resource can also be regarded as the referencing of a user to this resource, the tag–resource connections can be used for tag recommendations. This procedure resembles the recommending of co-occurring tags, but in this case it refers directly to the resource level and not, as in the first case, to the platform-specific folksonomy. The exploitation of neighbourhood in a social network looks at user similarity via co-tagged resources or co-used tags and can make suggestions for tag variants to the searching user. Alani et al. (2003) use social networks to offer synonyms to users, in particular. Wang and Davison (2008) use a variant of the Pseudo-Relevance feedback in order to enrich the user's search request with tags. They analyse the tags from an initial hit list of resources and offer these to the user for the purpose of query expansion.

The more elaborate variant of tag recommender systems is based on alignment with pre-existing KOS. Since the KOS reflect paradigmatic relations (Peters and Weller, 2008a), it is possible to create relational recommendations for query expansion in this way. This procedure is undoubtedly much more complex, since it involves constant alignment with and constant updating of the KOS. However, the user is offered the option of performing semantically correct modifications of the search request and of incorporating hyperonyms, hyponyms or synonyms via these recommender systems. Al-Khalifa and Davis (2006) suggest, for the use of relations in information retrieval, that the user can refine search requests during actual searches by selecting the desired relation (e.g. equivalence relation) from drop-down menus, thus expanding the search with synonyms. Query expansion via hyponyms is also addressed by Christiaens (2006). The connection of folksonomies and traditional methods of knowledge representation moves information retrieval closer to searches with controlled vocabularies, but does not involve too much effort for the user.

So far, there are only a few empirical studies on the use of recommender systems in folksonomies and on their use for information retrieval. The investigation by Jäschke et al. (2007), which observes the effects of recommended search tags on retrieval performance (via BibSonomy and Last.fm), is of note. When using recommendation methods the values of recall and precision are steadily increasing and as such are reflecting the enhancement of the retrieval quality.

Tag clouds facilitate browsing

The ability of folksonomies' to support browsing through information platforms rather than through specific searches via search forms and queries is often regarded as one of their great advantages. An effective and easily manageable browsing tool needs its own design criteria, rather than a simple search interface. This is why possibilities for visualizing folksonomies have been developed that go far beyond an alphabetical or list-oriented arrangement of tags (Hassan-Montero and Herrero-Solana, 2006).

In the visualization of folksonomies it is important for users to gain an impression of the information platform in its entirety and to find entry points for their browsing activities. Graphical interfaces are one way to provide this (Hassan-Montero and Herrero-Solana, 2006). Furthermore, browsing-compatible visualizations should reflect an order (Storey, 2007) so as to allow users to start searching more easily.

The best-known visualization method for folksonomies is tag clouds (Begelman, Keller and Smadja, 2006; Sinclair and Cardew-Hall, 2008; Bateman, Gutwin and Nacenta, 2008; Viégas and Wattenberg, 2008). Tag clouds consist either of the tags of a selected information resource or of the entire information platform's tags. The particularity of tag clouds is that they are arranged alphabetically (Figure 5.2).

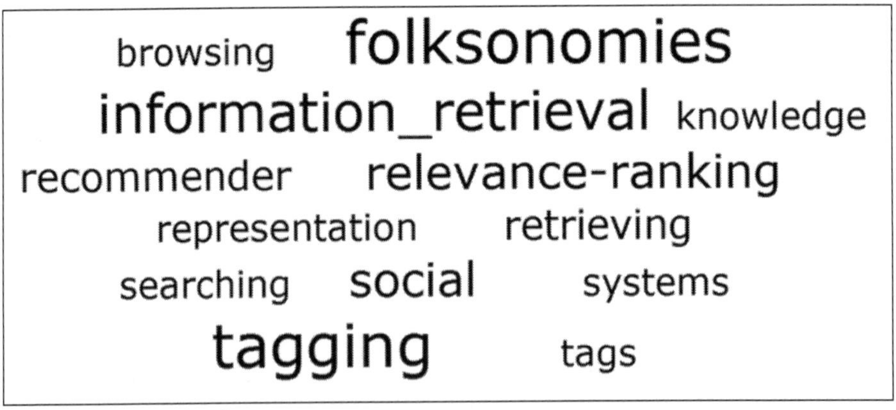

browsing **folksonomies**

information_retrieval knowledge

recommender **relevance-ranking**

representation retrieving

searching social systems

tagging tags

Figure 5.2 *Tag cloud*

The size of a tag is determined by its popularity on the resource or platform level (Bateman, Gutwin, and Nacenta, 2008), i.e. the more times the tag has been allocated, the larger it appears (Dye, 2006). Tag clouds thus show three dimensions of the folksonomy at the same time: tags, tag relevance and the alphabetical arrangement of the folksonomy (Hearst and Rosner, 2008). This visualization method is capable of providing users with access to the content of the information resource or platform at first glance, via the tags' semantics and their gradation according to frequency (Quintarelli, Resmini and Rosati, 2007; Viégas and Wattenberg, 2008).

Furthermore, trends in language use (Hearst and Rosner, 2008) and points of interest (Fichter, 2006) within the information platform or a community can be observed via tag size. Since Web 2.0 services make increasingly more content accessible to users, Viégas and Wattenberg (2008) see a great user need for structured means of representing textual resources, in particular, and they assume that this is the reason for the success of tag clouds. They present a 'friendly' environment, make visible the people behind the platform and invite users to browse through the website. Since tag clouds are mostly restricted to a certain number of tags, the user can quickly register the most important tags and use them as a browsing entry without first having to read and scroll through long lists (Hearst and Rosner, 2008). Tag clouds are thus an extremely comfortable browsing instrument (Hearst and Rosner, 2008). In particular, the option of quickly registering the information resource's context accounts for the attraction and popularity of tag clouds: 'With a tag cloud . . . users won't get a specific result, but what they will get is a very specific context of a subject. It saves a lot of reading. The content is the tag' (Dye, 2006, 42).

Apart from these important advantages, tag clouds also have flaws. Thus, the alphabetical arrangement of the tags often goes unnoticed by users (Hearst and Rosner, 2008). Users mainly orient themselves on the popular, larger tags and disregard others as browsing entries. On the other hand, tag clouds do not provide any visual constants, neglecting the 'natural visual flow' (Hearst and Rosner, 2008) that facilitates the registering of a text. Furthermore, the structure of the tags does not permit any conclusions to be drawn concerning relations or other semantic systematics between them, and so tag clouds ignore a potent retrieval functionality (Hassan-Montero and Herrero-Solana, 2006). Similar terms or descriptions within a tag cloud can be located quite far apart from each other, so that important associations go unmade, or even false links are created (Hearst and Rosner, 2008; Viégas and Wattenberg, 2008). Quintarelli, Resmini and Rosati (2007) locate the disadvantages resulting from tag clouds' lack of systematic arrangement in the language variability issue; the preference of frequent tags; the alphabetical arrangement of tags, which limits the possibilities of navigation; and the lack of visualization of the tags' semantic relatedness.

There are several approaches to overcoming the lack of systematic arrangement of tag clouds, mainly involving the introduction of semantic relatedness between tags (Hassan-Montero and Herreo-Solana, 2006) and cluster algorithms (Begelman, Keller and Smadja, 2006; Knautz, 2008; Knautz, Soubusta and Stock, 2010).

The representation of tags as dependent on their indexing frequency is another disadvantage of tag clouds. Tags with equal or similar font size are hard to compare or differentiate, so that users can find it difficult to determine the most relevant tags (Hearst and Rosner, 2008). Furthermore, the most popular tags are not always the most relevant, and so the tag cloud may reflect a false picture of the resource or platform. The same applies to the limited screen space, which hides a lot of tags from sight (Sen et al., 2007). The combination of relatively long words and large type can also make assessing a tag's relevance more difficult: 'indicating a word's importance by size causes problems. The length of the word is conflated with its size, thus making its importance seem to be a functional part of the number of characters it contains' (Hearst and Rosner, 2008). The effect of font size on users' judgement becomes noticeable in the subject coverage of tag clouds. Less popular subjects, such as the tags in the long tail, are less regarded by users and are thus used less often for indexing and searching (Hearst and Rosner, 2008). What is more, since a user can only ever search for one tag at a time in tag clouds, the retrieval power of tag clouds is fairly restricted (Hearst and Rosner, 2008).

The application of this assumption was the subject of several studies regarding the retrieval effectiveness of tag clouds. Sinclair and Cardew-Hall (2008) found that a tag cloud is mainly used as a retrieval tool in two cases: 1) far-reaching and unspecific search requests, and 2) search requests in which the search tag is displayed in the tag cloud. Also, searching via tag clouds can point up related articles or tags more effectively and thus reduces the user's cognitive effort in generating search terms. Regarding this point, it also becomes clear that users are more likely to use a tag cloud for search purposes when the desired search tag is displayed in the tag cloud than when it is not.

Tag clouds are also suited for searching by non-native speakers because they provide helpful suggestions for searching. Using the search field, on the other hand, is better suited to a concrete information need and also requires fewer steps to find the relevant article. Rivadeneira et al. (2007) focus on the different design elements of tag clouds. The authors found that tags with a large font size could be reproduced better than tags in smaller type. Also, tags from the upper left quadrant of the tag cloud were more easily memorized than those in the other quadrants. Here it may be observed that simple arrangements of the tags as lists, sorted by tag popularity, achieved the best results. The 'content' of tag clouds was registered even more effectively if the list-like arrangement of tags was complemented by larger font sizes for popular tags. Bateman, Gutwin and Nacenta (2008) respond to the study by Rivadeneira et al. (2007), but add further design criteria of tag clouds to their study. They conclude that the font size has the greatest influence on users and allows tags to appear to be very important. The font weighting and intensity, with regard to contrast, also have an important bearing on a tag's perceived relevance, whereas the number of a tag's pixels, as well as its width and area, have little influence on users, the colour of the text has pretty much no effect, and the tag's positioning influences the frequency with which it is selected (tags at the top and bottom edges of the tag cloud were selected less often than tags in the centre).

Relevance ranking

Relevance ranking in collaborative information services has long been – compared with other research endeavours – neglected in scientific debate (with the exception of Hotho et al., 2006c). These services themselves also do not (yet) place any great value on the ranking of search results: Connotea has no apparent ranking; Delicious ranks bookmarks reverse-chronologically according to their date of entry into the system and ranks tags according to their popularity (Szekely and Torres, 2005; Sturtz, 2004). On YouTube, users can at least arrange search results according to the relevance of criteria, date of entry, rating and view count. Gradually, more and more researchers and developers, as well as information services, are becoming aware of the necessity of a ranking mechanism: '[a]s these systems are growing, the currently implemented navigation by browsing tag clouds, with subsequent lists of bookmarks that are represented in chronological order, may not be the best arrangement for concise information retrieval' (Krause, Hotho and Stumme, 2008, 101). There is, in particular, a need to find distinctions between the relevant and less relevant resources in the growing mass of information on the platforms – ideally, by getting the top result for the query to appear at the very top of the hit list: 'ranking should be of highest priority for any community interested in providing information access and archival features' (Szekely and Torres, 2005).

Since the resources of collaborative information services often have links, link-topographical algorithms can be applied to them; they have the same problems with regard to ranking, however. That is why new methods of ranking are tested in folksonomies, since they open up new vistas for search engines and relevance ranking in their capacity as Web 2.0 components with their own characteristic features. The current approaches often combine folksonomies with known search engine methods and ranking algorithms, so as to implement the greatest advantages for determining relevant resources.

Bao et al. (2007) try to implement this combination with two different ranking algorithms within folksonomies. The 'SocialSimRank' is a query-dependent ranking factor that uses tags as the basis for comparison. The second ranking factor, 'SocialPageRank', is static in nature and calculates a resource's retrieval-status value not via its degree of linkage but via its number of tags. Richardson, Prakash and Brill (2006) introduce 'fRank', which is defined as a combination of RankNet and different features, where 'RankNet is a straightforward modification to the standard neural network back-prop algorithm' (2006, 709).

The innovation of this ranking algorithm is that the combined features (which are otherwise mostly used for a dynamic ranking) are tried for static ranking in this case. The ranking algorithms 'TagRank' and 'UserRank' (Szekely and Torres, 2005) modify the PageRank algorithm and serve to locate the best user and the best tag within the folksonomy. The UserRank incorporates user activity into its calculations and rewards the user who first annotates a popular tag for a resource. The TagRank works as follows: 'the rank of a tag is simply the sum of the UserRank of the tagger over all instances of the tag. This approach is based on the belief that the most relevant tags are those used by the best users' (Szekely and Torres, 2005). Ranking according to best or most relevant user is also aimed at by John and Seligmann (2006) in introducing 'ExpertRank'. The ExpertRank also incorporates user activity into its calculations to determine the most important user in the tagging community. It can be assumed that a user becomes more important the more resources he tags. The 'SBRank' by Yanbe et al. (2007) also follows the approach of combining the PageRank algorithm with users' collaboration in order to be able to provide a better search engine and a better ranking.

One of the few ranking algorithms already implemented in a collaborative information service is the 'FolkRank' (Hotho et al., 2006b). It is used in the scientifically oriented social bookmarking service BibSonomy. Hotho et al. (2006c; see also Hotho et al., 2006b, 2006d) were among the first to recognize the necessity of retrieval and ranking methods in tagging systems. The authors also orient themselves on PageRank's procedure (including Random Surfer) and start from the following assumption: 'The basic notion is that a resource which is tagged with important tags by important users becomes important itself' (Hotho et al., 2006c, 417). Also already implemented in a collaborative information service is the 'Interestingness Ranking' of the photo platform Flickr (Dennis, 2006; Liu et al., 2009). In a patent application for Flickr by Yahoo!, Butterfield et al. (2006a, 2006b) describe the meaning and purpose of a folksonomy-based Interestingness Ranking for multimedia resources. For a ranking according to the resource's 'interestingness' in Flickr, six general (1 to 6) and two personalized (7 and 8) criteria for determining the retrieval status value of a resource are defined:

1 *Click rates.*
2 *Extent of metadata*: how many items of metadata have been added to the resource?
3 *Number of tagging users and tag popularity.*
4 *Tag relevance*: is the tag deemed relevant by the users or not (via active user ratings)?
5 *Chronology*: the algorithm reduces a resource's retrieval-status value by

2% per tag each day after it has been entered.

6   *Relation between the metadata*: what tags co-occur the most?

7   *Relation between author and user:* registered users and registered authors are potentially more similar.

8   *Relation between location and residence*: the locally nearer a tagged or saved object is to the user's residence, the more relevant it is for him.

The ranking factors suggested by Yahoo! purposefully exploit the collaborative aspects of the tagging systems, but by a long way do not exhaust all ranking possibilities – in particular, traditional retrieval models such as the Vector-Space model or the link topology and the user's concrete search and indexing behaviour are not taken into consideration. Another problem for the Interestingness Ranking is the factor 'time'. It is not necessarily always the case that a resource decreases in relevance over time. If it were so, the relevance of Michelangelo's *Mona Lisa*, for instance, would be near zero today – which might very well be disputed by art historians.

The ranking possibilities for resources within folksonomies can generally be concentrated into three main areas or feature sets: tags, collaboration and users (Figure 5.3). Each area consists of individual ranking factors which can each be weighted separately in order to give certain aspects stronger or weaker

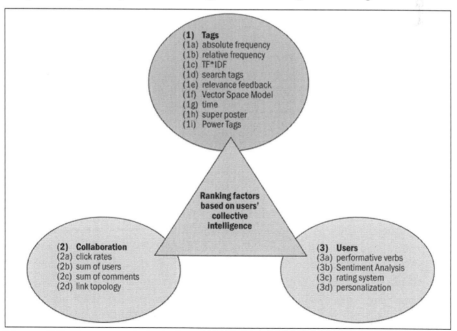

Figure 5.3 *Three sets of criteria for relevance ranking in and with folksonomies (Peters, 2009, 345, Figure 4.24)*

consideration in the ranking, i.e. to affect the resource's retrieval status value (RSV) positively (rise) or negatively (drop). The feature set 'tags' is query dependent, i.e. there must be a match between search term and indexing term and the resource's RSV must be calculated anew for each search request. The feature sets 'collaboration' and 'user' are query independent, which means that the resource's RSV is not calculated with regard to the search request but remains the same for each resource. The retrieval status of each resource can be made up of either the consideration of the individual ranking factors or the summarization of the individual feature sets. This generates the RSV of each resource, which is used as the basis of the relevance ranking. Exactly which form of RSV measurement will yield an adequate result in each respective case must be determined through empirical observation.

The first feature set considers the concrete tags of the folksonomy and processes them for relevance ranking. Since the ranking refers to the resource level, it is important to stress at this point that the entire bundle of criteria 'tags' can be applied only in Broad Folksonomies (Vander Wal, 2005b), since they allow for resource-specific tag distributions.

The second criteria bundle incorporates users' active collaboration, i.e. the behaviour of individual users added to the respective resource, into the ranking as positive factors (Agichtein, Brill and Dumais, 2006; Gou et al., 2010; Joachims, 2002; Kashoob, Caverlee and Kamath, 2010; Xue et al., 2004). Tonkin et al. (2008) may still ask: 'Amazon and Google use personal information to generate popularity or relevance indicators, do non-subject tags offer any similar advantages?'; but the following remarks will show that most of the different sorts of collaboration, even from the area of search engine analysis and others, can be implemented for the ranking. The elements of this feature set here work query-independently, meaning that they are formed from resource-inherent factors and ascribe a value to the resource.

The third set of ranking criteria refers to the user and his conscious acts. In contrast to click data, which only implicitly reflect use behaviour, these ranking factors are explicitly and actively designed by the users. The factors presented here are query independent, just as in the previous feature set.

The fact that the user can also actively participate in the ranking and receive opportunities to leave feedback should not go unmentioned at this point. This can occur via the traditional Relevance Feedback (e.g. Rocchio, 1971). The advantage of the Relevance Feedback is that the initial query (often consisting of very few tags) is enhanced by further tags from the positively marked resources. The Vector-Space model, in particular, benefits from this query expansion because it requires many dimensions for evaluation in order to provide an ideal search result. The Relevance Feedback occurs after an initial search and can be performed over several rounds, on the basis of each new respective search term and the ranking factors mentioned above (Yin et al., 2010).

From the perspective of users, it is important that they be able to turn off such sophisticated ranking algorithms, either wholly or partially (Stock, 2007b). A drop-down menu seems to be the ideal method for including users in the process of adjusting the ranking factors in order to arrange search results. Users can then decide for themselves by what criteria they want the results to be arranged and displayed. Perhaps they prefer formal criteria (date of publication, author etc.), or only very specific criteria from the relevance-ranking toolbox. All user needs could be satisfied this way.

Tagging systems offer a wealth of ranking options that go beyond the traditional methods of database providers and web searches (Morrison, 2008). Hammond et al. (2005) thus conclude: 'when it comes to ranking by relevance (as opposed to merely identifying potentially relevant resources), this kind of data might actually be more useful than a much smaller number of tightly controlled keywords'.

Ranking algorithms are not immune from attacks and manipulation by spammers. Ranking factors that are based on the mere indexing frequency of tags are particularly susceptible. A first step to avoiding spam, especially with regard to this aspect, is the saving of tagging users' IP addresses. The multiple indexing of the same tags from one IP address should thus be, if not prevented outright, at the very least made more difficult. Amazon already uses this form of spam obstruction and does not register a tag indexed more than once in the resource's folksonomy – but without alerting the user that he has already indexed this tag for that resource.

Disadvantages

The disadvantages of information retrieval with folksonomies are mainly the same as in knowledge representation, and result from the lack of a controlled vocabulary. The weaknesses of folksonomies are particularly apparent here, since users may not be presented with any resources in response to their query, or the hit list may consist of irrelevant resources. The immediate connection between the areas of knowledge representation and information retrieval is probably more evident for users here than anywhere else.

Just as in knowledge representation, methods for unifying search terms and creating semantic unambiguousness can also be used in information retrieval. The search tags can also be processed information-linguistically, for example, in order to generate a greater probability of matches between searching and indexing vocabulary (Guy and Tonkin, 2006). Query expansion via semantic relations can also support the finding of relevant resources, since these present the user with alternative search terms. More general search terms, i.e. tags on higher levels of the term ladder, provide for a higher recall, while more specific search tags on lower term-hierarchy levels restrict it, thus raising the search results' precision. Since folksonomies do not yet use either of the two options for information retrieval, their retrieval functionality resembles search in full text (Weinberger, 2005) and is not yet fully pronounced. The entire search effort is passed on to the user; after all, the user is the one who must think about all linguistic variants of a term and manually enter them into the search field in order to achieve the most complete search result possible. The eventual problem of homonyms has not been considered, though, which leads to possible ballast in the hit list. Folksonomies are thus badly suited for both recall-oriented research and precision-oriented research.

The motto of many popular tagging systems appears to be 'quantity, not quality' with regard to their retrieval effectiveness. Morrison (2008, 1563) observes that users (particularly information professionals) should accept that folksonomies are not a formidable retrieval tool: 'It is important to note that Web sites that employ folksonomies [. . .] are not necessarily designed to have search as the primary goal'. Consequently, collaborative information services have not been developed for better information gathering but seem primarily to follow other goals. Networking of users based on different resources and the decentralized storage of personal and already-found resources are in the foreground; the finding of interesting information and resources is merely a pleasant side-effect.

If a resource in a tagging system has been indexed with tags, this does not mean that the resource is actually relevant to the tag (Koutrika et al., 2007). Since there is no quality control with regard to the allocation of resources and tags in folksonomies, inadequate or simply false indexing can occur. This fact is exploited by spammers for 'spagging', in which they terrorize the tagging system with unsuitable tag-resource links (Szekely and Torres, 2005), with the result that search users receive inordinate amounts of ballast in response to their queries.

Another definite limit of folksonomies is their dependence on the collaborative information service. Generally, folksonomies can be searched for only one information platform; no provision is made for a 'cross-platform' or 'universal search'. More and more meta search engines are appearing that make it possible for users to search the folksonomies of different platforms at the same time and to retrieve the different resources as search results. The meta search engine MyTag (http://mytag.uni-koblenz.de) (Braun et al., 2008) allows parallel searches in Flickr, Delicious and YouTube. A personalized ranking of the search results via the user personomy is also possible. TagsAhoy (www.tagsahoy.com) proceeds in a similar manner and allows users to search only their own personomy within the services Delicious, Flickr, Gmail, Squirl, LibraryThing and Connotea.

So far, there have been only a few studies on user searching behaviour within and with folksonomies. To get an impression of the usability of folksonomies with regard to their retrieval functionality, one must consult related studies instead. Van Hooland (2006) analyses users' queries within the image database of the Dutch National Archive via the Shatford Classification (who, what, when, specific, generic, abstract). Van Hooland (2006), as well as Rorissa (2008), is able to show that when it comes to the degree of tag specificity, there is mostly a match between indexing and search vocabulary. Small deviations are merely detectable in the fact that users tend to index on the specific or instance level (e.g. the tag 'me') and the basic level while conversely searching on all three levels (subordinate, basic level, superordinate) (Rosch, 1975). A complete overlap is noticeable only in the lack of indexing tags and query tags on the very abstract level. After the grammatical and semantic cleansing of both vocabularies it thus becomes possible for users to find the desired resources even via folksonomies.

Conclusion

Unanswered research questions on the subjects of folksonomies and information retrieval are concerned mainly with the design of search engines for collaborative information services, the visualization of search results, the measuring of the success of folksonomies and tagging systems, and the exploitation of user activity for information retrieval.

In search engine development the question arises as to whether a 'one size fits all' solution could be possible, i.e. the development of a search engine for all resource types throughout the different collaborative information services, or whether different specialized search engines meet users' needs in searching for information more effectively. Hearst, Hurst and Dumais (2008) see an advantage for specialized search engines that are able to adapt perfectly to resource-specific characteristics and retrieval demands and suggest the creation of a blog search engine that works with facets. The facets should cover aspects such as blog genre or frequency of update and make them available for information retrieval.

The visualization of search results has also not yet been discussed. The advantages and disadvantages of tag clouds are sufficiently investigated and numerous improved display options are presented, but:

> Few Web applications do anything to organize or to summarize the contents of such responses beyond ranking the items in the list [. . .] and are generally not provided with any way to visualize the totality of the results returned.
>
> (Kuo et al., 2007, 1203)

Fichter and Wisniewski (2008) remark that measurement of the success of collaborative information services has not been discussed yet. If anyone wants to determine their success via the effectiveness of their folksonomies, I would refer them to the conceptual approach by Furner (2007). Here the success criteria for folksonomies and tagging systems are discussed in great detail and suggestions for the development of an evaluation system are made. The joint venture Social Media (AG Social Media, 2009) is leading initial discussions towards establishing a 'social media currency' that is intended to consist of range and intensity measurements. Bertram (2009) criticizes users' lack of maintenance in tagging systems and folksonomies, as hardly anyone repairs resources once they have been saved or deletes an invalid URL, e.g. in social bookmarking. The Tag Gardening (Peters and Weller, 2008b) tool 'tagCare' (Golov, Weller, and Peters, 2008) has been introduced, which is capable of meeting this criticism, at least in personal resource management and personal tag maintenance. Yoo and Suh (2010) also allow for the free definition of tag categories to structure folksonomies according to users' needs.

Ranking of resources in tagging systems and evaluation of the adequacy of tags for resources are also still open for research. A method for enhancing the precision of search results works with so-called 'power tags', which eliminate all tags of the resource-specific long tail (Peters and Stock, 2010). The approach of Liu et al. (2009) ranks tags according to their relevance to an image and presents a way to create a tag ranking in narrow folksonomies that may otherwise rely on search tag distributions (Peters, 2009). The relevance of tags and their disambiguation in order to improve search results are discussed by Li, Snoek and Worring (2008) and Weinberger, Slaney and Van Zwol (2008).

Smith et al. (2008) formulate the six requirements (1) 'filter', (2) 'rank', (3) 'disambiguate', (4) 'share', (5) 'recommend' and (6) 'matchmake' for folksonomies. From the examples in this chapter, it can be observed that the first four are not being met in practice, as of yet. An exception is Flickr's Interestingness Ranking, which implements parts of the requirements in its algorithm. The last two requirements, 'recommend' and 'matchmake', are entirely met by folksonomies and collaborative information services. A prototypical example would be Amazon, but LibraryThing, for instance, also makes heavy use of the recommendation options of folksonomies. At this point, the aspect of recommendations based on the identical tags of two users not exclusively being generated automatically but reflecting user participation is important. The significance for e-commerce is defined by Dye (2006, 43):

> Human-generated metadata [. . .] can be more valuable than that generated by a robot. For marketing towards the Internet community, insight into the consumer's thought process can be priceless. That's why [. . .] Internet commerce sites are

exploring how to incorporate tagging into their interfaces. [. . .] Amazon can generate recommendations for other items based on users' tags.

Over the course of this chapter, it has been shown that folksonomies are suited for social search, where their strengths lie mainly in the areas of relevance ranking and social browsing (Brusilovsky, 2008), as the following extract confirms:

> What is social search? [. . .] Simply put, social search tools are internet wayfinding services informed by human judgement. Wayfinding, because they're not strictly search engines [. . .] And human judgement means that [. . .] people have 'consumed' the content and have decided it's worthy enough to recommend to others.
>
> (Sherman, 2006)

According to Evans and Chi (2008), social interaction plays an important part in all stages of research. On this basis, they endorse the use of folksonomy and all of its facets (such as social navigation or collaborative recommender systems) in information retrieval because folksonomies maintain the visibility of the users of collaborative information services and their availability for social interaction at all times.

It is clear, then, that users and their activity play an important role in collaborative information services and folksonomies. It is through the users that the traditional information retrieval of libraries and the internet is being transformed into 'Information Retrieval 2.0'.

Note

This contribution is an updated summary of the chapter 'Information Retrieval with Folksonomies' from Peters (2009), *Folksonomies: indexing and retrieval in Web 2.0*, De Gruyter Saur.

References

AG Social Media (2009) Ergebnisse des Measurement Summits, http://ag-sm.de/?p=116.

Agichtein, E., Brill, E. and Dumais, S. (2006) Improving Web Search Ranking by Incorporating User Behaviour Information. In *Proceedings of the 29th Annual International ACM SIGIR Conference on Research and Development in Information Retrieval, Seattle, USA*, 19–26.

Alani, H., Dasmahapatra, S., O'Hara, K. and Shadbolt, N. (2003) Identifying Communities of Practice through Ontology Network Analysis, *IEEE Intelligent Systems*, **18** (2), 18–25.

Al-Khalifa, H. S. and Davis, H. C. (2006) FolksAnnotation: a semantic metadata tool for annotating learning resources using folksonomies and domain ontologies. In *Proceedings of the 2nd International IEEE Conference on Innovations in Information Technology, Dubai, UAE*.

Auray, N. (2007) Folksonomy: the new way to serendipity, *Communications & Strategies*, **65**, 67–89.

Bao, S. et al. (2007) Optimizing Web Search Using Social Annotations. In *Proceedings of the 16th International WWW Conference, Banff, Alberta, Canada*, 501–10.

Bateman, S., Gutwin, C. and Nacenta, M. (2008) Seeing Things in the Clouds: the effect of visual features on tag cloud selections. In *Proceedings of the 19th ACM Conference on Hypertext and Hypermedia, Pittsburgh, PA, USA*, 193–202.

Begelman, G., Keller, P. and Smadja, F. (2006) Automated Tag Clustering: improving search and exploration in the tag space. In *Proceedings of the Collaborative Web Tagging Workshop at WWW 2006, Edinburgh, Scotland*.

Bertram, J. (2009) Social Tagging: zum Potential einer neuen Indexiermethode, *Information – Wissenschaft & Praxis*, **60** (1), 19–26.

Bischoff, K., Firan, C. S., Nejdl, W. and Paiu, R. (2010) Bridging the Gap between Tagging and Querying Vocabularies: analyses and applications for enhancing multimedia IR, *Web Semantics: Science, Services and Agents on the World Wide Web*, 8(2–3), 97–109.

Blank, M., Bopp, T., Hampel, T. and Schulte, J. (2008) Social Tagging = Soziale Suche? In Gaiser, B., Hampel, T. and Panke, S. (eds), *Good Tags – Bad Tags: Social Tagging in der Wissensorganisation: Vol. 47, Medien in der Wissenschaft*, Waxmann.

Braun, M., Dellschaft, K., Franz, T., Hering, D., Jungen, P., Metzler, H. et al. (2008) Personalized Search and Exploration with MyTag. In *Proceedings of the 17th International Conference on World Wide Web, Beijing, China*, 1031–2.

Brooks, C. and Montanez, N. (2006a) An Analysis of the Effectiveness of Tagging in Blogs. In Nicolov, N., Salvetti, F., Liberman, M. and Martin, J. (eds), *Computation Approaches to Analyzing Weblogs: papers from the 2006 AAAI Spring Symposium*, AAAI Press, 9–15.

Brooks, C. and Montanez, N. (2006b) Improved Annotation of the Blogosphere via Autotagging and Hierarchical Clustering. In *Proceedings of the Collaborative Web Tagging Workshop at WWW 2006, Edinburgh, Scotland*.

Brusilovsky, P. (2008) Social Information Access: the other side of the social web, *Lecture Notes in Computer Science*, **4910**, 5–22.

Butterfield, D., Costello, E., Fake, C., Henderson-Begg, C. and Mourachow, S. (2006b) Interestingness Ranking of Media Objects, US Patent No. US 2006/0242139.

Butterfield, D., Costello, E., Fake, C., Henderson-Begg, C., Mourachow, S. and Schachter, J. (2006a) Media Object Metadata Association and Ranking, US Patent No. US 2006/0242178A1.

Capocci, A. and Caldarelli, G. (2008) Folksonomies and Clustering in the Collaborative

System CiteULike, *Journal of Physics A: Mathematical and Theoretical*, **41**, http://arxiv.org/abs/0710.2835.

Chen, H. (1994) Collaborative Systems: solving the vocabulary problem, *IEEE Computer, Special Issue on Computer-Supported Cooperative Work*, **27** (5), 58–66.

Chi, E. H. and Mytkowicz, T. (2006) Understanding Navigability of Social Tagging Systems, www.viktoria.se/altchi/submissions/submission_edchi_0.pdf.

Chopin, K. (2008) Finding Communities: alternative viewpoints through weblogs and tagging, *Journal of Documentation*, **64** (4), 552–75.

Choy, S. and Lui, A. K. (2006). Web Information Retrieval in Collaborative Tagging Systems. In *Proceedings of the IEEE/WIC/ACM International Conference on Web Intelligence, Hong Kong*, 352–55.

Christiaens, S. (2006) Metadata Mechanism: from ontology to folksonomy . . . and back, *Lecture Notes in Computer Science*, **4277**, 199–207.

Cox, A., Clough, P. and Marlow, J. (2008) Flickr: a first look at user behaviour in the context of photography as serious leisure, *Information Research*, **13** (1), http://informationr.net/ir/13-1/paper336.html.

Crawford, W. (2006) Folksonomy and Dichotomy, *Cites & Insights: Crawford at Large*, **6** (4), cites.boisestate.edu/civ6i4.pdf.

Cui, H., Wen, J. R., Nie, J. Y. and Ma, W. Y. (2002) Probabilistic Query Expansion Using Query Logs. In *Proceedings of the 11th International Conference on World Wide Web, Honolulu, Hawaii, USA*, 325–32.

Dennis, B. M. (2006) Foragr: collaboratively tagged photographs and social information visualization. In *Proceedings of the Collaborative Web Tagging Workshop at WWW 2006, Edinburgh, Scotland.*

Dieberger, A. (1997) Supporting Social Navigation on the World Wide Web, *International Journal of Human–Computer Studies*, **46** (6), 805–25.

Dieberger, A., Dourish, P., Höök, K., Resnick, P. and Wexelblat, A. (2000) Social Navigation: techniques for building more usable systems, *Interactions*, **7** (6), 36–45.

Diederich, J. and Iofciu, T. (2006) Finding Communities of Practice from User Profiles Based on Folksonomies. In Tomadaki, E. and Scott, P. (eds), *Innovative Approaches for Learning and Knowledge Sharing, EC-TEL 2006 Workshops Proceedings, Crete, Greece*, 288–97.

Ding, Y., Jacob, E. K., Zhang, Z., Foo, S., Yan, E., George, N. L. and Guo, L. (2009) Perspectives on Social Tagging, *Journal of the American Society for Information Science and Technology*, **60** (12), 2388–401.

Dye, J. (2006) Folksonomy: a game of high-tech (and high-stakes) tag, *EContent*, April, 38–43.

Efthimiadis, E. N. (1996) Query Expansion, *Annual Review of Information Science and Technology*, **31**, 121–87.

Efthimiadis, E. N. (2000) Interactive Query Expansion: a user-based evaluation in a relevance feedback environment, *Journal of the American Society for Information*

Science and Technology, **51**, 989–1003.

Evans, B. M. and Chi, E. H. (2008) Towards a Model of Understanding Social Search. In Soboroff, I., Agichtein, E. and Kumar, R. (eds), *Proceedings of the 2008 ACM Workshop on Search in Social Media, Napa Valley, California,* 83–6.

Farrell, S., Lau, T., Wilcox, E. and Muller, M. J. (2007) Socially Augmenting Employee Profiles with People-tagging. In *Proceedings of the 20th Annual ACM Symposium on User Interface Software and Technology, Newport, Rhode Island, USA,* 91–100.

Feldman, S. (2000) Find What I Mean, Not What I Say: meaning-based search tools, *Online – Leading Magazine for Information Professionals,* **24** (3), 49–56.

Fichter, D. (2006) Intranet Applications for Tagging and Folksonomies, *Online – Leading Magazine for Information Professionals,* **30** (3), 43–5.

Fichter, D. and Wisniewski, J. (2008) Social Media Metrics: making the case for making the effort, *Online,* November/December, **32** (6), 54–7.

Fokker, J., Pouwelse, J. and Buntine, W. (2006) Tag-Based Navigation for Peer-to-Peer Wikipedia. In *Proceedings of the Collaborative Web Tagging Workshop at WWW 2006, Edinburgh, Scotland.*

Forsberg, M., Höök, K. and Svensson, M. (1998) Design Principles for Social Navigation Tools. In *Proceedings of the 4th ERCIM Workshop on User Interfaces for All, Stockholm, Sweden.*

Freyne, J. and Smyth B. (2004) An Experiment in Social Search, *Lecture Notes in Computer Science,* **3137**, 95–103.

Freyne, J., Farzan R., Brusilovsky P., Smyth B. and Coyle M. (2007) Collecting Community Wisdom: integrating social search and social navigation. In *Proceedings of the International Conference on Intelligent User Interfaces, Honolulu, Hawaii, USA,* 52–61.

Fu, W. T., Kannampallil, T., Kang, R. and He, J. (2010) Semantic Imitation in Social Tagging, *ACM Transactions on Computer–Human Interaction,* **17** (3), article 12.

Furnas, G., Landauer, T., Gomez, L. and Dumais, S. (1987) The Vocabulary Problem in Human–System Communication, *Communications of the ACM,* **30** (11), 964–71.

Furner, J. (2007) User Tagging of Library Resources: toward a framework for system evaluation. In *Proceedings of World Library and Information Congress, Durban, South Africa.*

Golov, E., Weller, K. and Peters, I. (2008) TagCare: a personal portable tag repository. In *Proceedings of the Poster and Demonstration Session at the 7th International Semantic Web Conference, Karlsruhe, Germany.*

Goodrum, A. and Spink, A. (2001) Image Searching on the Excite Web Search Engine, *Information Processing and Management,* **37** (2), 295–311.

Gordon-Murnane, L. (2006) Social Bookmarking, Folksonomies, and Web 2.0 Tools, *Searcher – The Magazine for Database Professionals,* **14** (6), 26–38.

Gou, L., Zhang, X. L., Chen, H. H., Kim, J. H. and Giles, C. L. (2010) Social Network Document Ranking. In *Proceedings of the 10th Annual Joint Conference on Digital*

Libraries, Gold Coast, Australia, 313–22.

Graham, R., Eoff, B. and Caverlee, J. (2008) Plurality: a context-aware personalized tagging system. In *Proceedings of the 17th International Conference on World Wide Web, Beijing, China*, 1165–6.

Grahl, M., Hotho, A. and Stumme, G. (2007) Conceptual Clustering of Social Bookmarking Sites. In Tochtermann, K. and Maurer, H. (eds), *Proceedings of I-KNOW, 7th International Conference on Knowledge Management, Graz, Austria*, JUCS (Journal of Universal Computer Science), 356–64.

Greenberg, J. (2001) Automatic Query Expansion via Lexical-Semantic Relationships, *Journal of the American Society for Information Science and Technology*, **52** (5), 402–15.

Gruber, T. (2005) Ontology of Folksonomy: a mash-up of apples and oranges, www.tomgruber.org/writing/mtsr05-ontology-of-folksonomy.htm.

Guy, M. and Tonkin, E. (2006) Folksonomies: tidying up tags? *D-Lib Magazine*, **12** (1).

Hammond, T., Hannay, T., Lund, B. and Scott, J. (2005) Social Bookmarking Tools (I), *D-Lib Magazine* **11** (4).

Hassan-Montero, Y. and Herrero-Solana, V. (2006) Improving Tag-clouds as Visual Information Retrieval Interfaces. In *Proceedings of the International Conference on Multidisciplinary Information Science and Technologies, Mérida, Spain*.

Hearst, M. and Rosner, D. (2008) Tag Clouds: data analysis tool or social signaller? In *Proceedings of the 41st Hawaii International Conference on System Sciences*.

Hearst, M. A., Hurst, M. and Dumais, S. T. (2008) What Should Blog Search Look Like? In Soboroff, I., Agichtein, E. and Kumar, R. (eds), *Proceedings of the 2008 ACM Workshop on Search in Social Media, Napa Valley, California*, 95–8.

Heck, T. and Peters, I. (2010) Expert Recommender Systems: establishing communities of practice based on social bookmarking systems. In *Proceedings of I-Know 2010: 10th International Conference on Knowledge Management and Knowledge Technologies, Graz, Austria*, 458–64.

Heymann, P. and Garcia-Molina, H. (2006) *Collaborative Creation of Communal Hierarchical Taxonomies in Social Tagging Systems: InfoLab technical report*, http://dbpubs.stanford.edu/pub/2006-10.

Heymann, P., Paepcke, A. and Garcia-Molina, H. (2010) Tagging Human Knowledge. In *Proceedings of the 3rd ACM International Conference on Web Search and Data Mining, New York, USA*, 51–60.

Hotho, A., Jäschke, R., Schmitz, C. and Stumme, G. (2006a) Bibsonomy: a social bookmark and publication sharing system. In *Proceedings of the Conceptual Structure Tool Interoperability Workshop at the 14th International Conference on Conceptual Structures, Aalborg, Denmark*, 87–102.

Hotho, A., Jäschke, R., Schmitz, C. and Stumme, G. (2006b) FolkRank: a ranking algorithm for folksonomies. In Schaaf, M. and Althoff, K. D. (eds), *Proceedings of FGIR 2006: Workshop Information Retrieval 2006 of the Special Interest Group Information Retrieval, Hildesheim, Germany*.

Hotho, A., Jäschke, R., Schmitz, C. and Stumme, G. (2006c) Information Retrieval in Folksonomies: search and ranking, *Lecture Notes in Computer Science*, **4011**, 411–26.

Hotho, A., Jäschke, R., Schmitz, C. and Stumme, G. (2006d) Das Entstehen von Semantik in BibSonomy. In *Proceedings of Social Software in der Wertschöpfung, Baden-Baden, Germany.*

Jäschke, R., Marinho, L., Hotho, A., Schmidt-Thieme, L. and Stumme, G. (2007) Tag Recommendations in Folksonomies, *Lecture Notes in Artificial Intelligence*, **4702**, 506–14.

Joachims, T. (2002) Optimizing Search Engines Using Clickthrough Data. In *Proceedings of SIGKDD Edmonton, Alberta, Canada*, 133–42.

John, A. and Seligmann, D. (2006) Collaborative Tagging and Expertise in the Enterprise. In *Proceedings of the 15th International Conference on World Wide Web, Edinburgh, Scotland.*

Jörgensen, C. (2007) Image Access, the Semantic Gap, and Social Tagging as a Paradigm Shift. In *Proceedings of the 18th Workshop of the ASIS&T Special Interest Group in Classification Research, Milwaukee, Wisconsin, USA* (CD-ROM).

Kashoob, S., Caverlee, J. and Kamath, K. (2010) Community-based Ranking of the Social Web. In *Proceedings of the 21st ACM Conference on Hypertext and Hypermedia, Toronto, Canada*, 141–50.

Knautz, K. (2008) Von der Tag-Cloud zum Tag-Cluster: Statistischer Thesaurus auf der Basis syntagmatischer Relationen und seine mögliche Nutzung in Web 2.0-Diensten. In Ockenfeld, M. (ed.), *Verfügbarkeit von Informationen: Proceedings der 30. Online-Tagung der DGI, Frankfurt a.M., Germany*, DGI.

Knautz, K., Soubusta, S. and Stock, W. G. (2010) Tag Clusters as Information Retrieval Interfaces. In *Proceedings of the 43rd Annual Hawaii International Conference on System Sciences, Kauai, Hawaii.*

Koutrika, G., Effendi, F. A., Gyöngyi, P., Heymann, P. and Garcia-Molina, H. (2007) Combating Spam in Tagging Systems. In *Proceedings of the 3rd International Workshop on Adversarial Information Retrieval on the Web, Banff, Alberta, Canada*, 57–64.

Krause, B., Hotho, A. and Stumme, G. (2008) A Comparison of Social Bookmarking with Traditional Search. In *Proceedings of the 30th European Conference on IR Research, ECIR, Glasgow, Scotland*, 101–13.

Kuo, B. Y., Hentrich, T., Good, B. M., and Wilkinson, M. D. (2007) Tag Clouds for Summarizing Web Search Results. In *Proceedings of the 16th International WWW Conference, Banff, Alberta, Canada*, 1203–4.

Lambiotte, R. and Ausloos, M. (2006) Collaborative Tagging as a Tripartite Network, *Lecture Notes in Computer Science*, **3993**, 1114–17.

Lerman, K. and Jones, L. A. (2006) Social Browsing on Flickr, http://arxiv.org/abs/cs/0612047.

Li, X. R., Snoek, C. G. M. and Worring, M. (2008) Learning Tag Relevance by Neighbor:

voting for social image retrieval. In *Proceedings of the 16th ACM International Conference on Multimedia Information Retrieval, Vancouver, Canada.*

Liu, D., Hua, X. S., Yang, L., Wang, M. and Zhang, H. J. (2009) Tag Ranking. In *Proceedings of the 18th International Conference on World Wide Web, Madrid, Spain,* 351–60.

Marlow, C., Naaman, M., Boyd, D. and Davis, M. (2006a) HT06, Tagging Paper, Taxonomy, Flickr, Academic Article, To Read. In *Proceedings of the 17th Conference on Hypertext and Hypermedia, Odense, Denmark,* 31–40.

Marlow, C., Naaman, M., Boyd, D. and Davis, M. (2006b) Position Paper, Tagging, Taxonomy, Flickr, Article, ToRead. In *Proceedings of the Collaborative Web Tagging Workshop at WWW 2006, Edinburgh, Scotland.*

Mathes, A. (2004) Folksonomies: cooperative classification and communication through shared metadata, www.adammathes.com/academic/computer-mediated-communication/folksonomies.html.

Merton, R. K. (1949) *Social Theory and Social Structure,* The Free Press.

Millen, D. R., Feinberg, J. and Kerr, B. (2006) Dogear: social bookmarking in the enterprise. In *Proceedings of the Conference on Human Factors in Computing Systems, Montréal, Canada,* 111–20.

Millen, D. R., Whittaker, M. Y. S. and Feinberg, J. (2007) Social Bookmarking and Exploratory Search. In *Proceedings of the 10th European Conference on Computer-Supported Cooperative Work, Limerick, Ireland,* 21–40.

Mishne, G. (2006) AutoTag: a collaborative approach to automated tag assignment for weblog posts. In *Proceedings of the 15th International Conference on World Wide Web, Edinburgh, Scotland,* 953–54.

Mislove, A., Koppula, H. S., Gummadi, K. P., Druschel, P. and Bhattacharjee, B. (2008) Growth of the Flickr Social Network. In *Proceedings of the 1st Workshop on Online Social Networks, Seattle, WA, USA,* 25–30.

Morrison, P. (2008) Tagging and Searching: search retrieval effectiveness of folksonomies on the World Wide Web, *Information Processing & Management,* **44** (4), 1562–79.

Muller, M. J. (2007) Comparing Tagging Vocabularies among Four Enterprise Tag-Based Services. In *Proceedings of the International ACM Conference on Supporting Group Work, Sanibel Island, FL, USA,* 341–50.

Panke, S. and Gaiser, B. (2008) Nutzerperspektiven auf Social Tagging: eine Online Befragung, www.e-teaching.org/didaktik/recherche/goodtagsbadtags2.pdf.

Paolillo, J. and Penumarthy, S. (2007) The Social Structure of Tagging Internet Video on del.icio.us. In *Proceedings of the 40th Hawaii International Conference on System Sciences, Hawaii.*

Peters, I. (2009) *Folksonomies: indexing and retrieval in Web 2.0,* De Gruyter Saur.

Peters, I. and Stock, W. G. (2010) 'Power Tags' in Information Retrieval, *Library Hi Tech,* **28** (1), 81–93.

Peters, I. and Weller, K. (2008a) Paradigmatic and Syntagmatic Relations in Knowledge Organization Systems, *Information – Wissenschaft und Praxis*, **59** (2), 100–7.

Peters, I. and Weller, K. (2008b) Tag Gardening for Folksonomy Enrichment and Maintenance, *Webology*, **5** (3), article 58, www.webology.ir/2008/v5n3/a58.html.

Pluzhenskaia, M. (2006) Folksonomies or Fauxonomies: how social is social bookmarking? In *Proceedings of the 17th Annual ASIS&T SIG/CR Classification Research Workshop, Austin, Texas, USA* (CD-ROM).

Quintarelli, E., Resmini, A. and Rosati, L. (2007) Face Tag: integrating bottom-up and top-down classification in a social tagging system, *Bulletin of the ASIST*, **33** (5), 10–15.

Richardson, M., Prakash, A. and Brill, E. (2006) Beyond PageRank: machine learning for static ranking. In *Proceedings of the 15th International Conference on World Wide Web, Edinburgh, Scotland*, 707–15.

Rivadeniera, A. W., Gruen, D. M., Muller, M. J. and Millen, D. R. (2007) Getting Our Head in the Clouds: toward evaluation studies of tagclouds. In *Proceedings of the SIGCHI Conference on Human Factors in Computing Systems, San Jose, California, USA*, 995–8.

Rocchio, J. J. (1971) Relevance Feedback in Information Retrieval. In Salton, G. (ed.), *The SMART Retrieval System: experiments in automatic document processing*, Prentice Hall PTR.

Rorissa, A. (2008) User-generated Descriptions of Individual Images versus Labels of Groups of Images: a comparison using basic level theory, *Information Processing and Management*, **44** (5), 1741–53.

Rosch, E. (1975) Cognitive Reference Points, *Cognitive Psychology*, **7** (4), 532–47.

Sandusky, R. (2006) Shared Persistent User Search Paths: social navigation as social classification. In *Proceedings of the 17th Annual ASIS&T SIG/CR Classification Research Workshop, Austin, Texas, USA*.

Schillerwein, S. (2008) Der 'Business Case' für die Nutzung von Social Tagging in Intranets und internen Informationssystemen. In Gaiser, B., Hampel, T. and Panke, S. (eds), *Good Tags – Bad Tags: Social Tagging in der Wissensorganisation: Vol. 47, Medien in der Wissenschaft*, Waxmann.

Sen, S., Harper, F., LaPitz, A. and Riedl, J. (2007) The Quest for Quality Tags. In *Proceedings of the International ACM Conference on Supporting Group Work, Sanibel Island, FL, USA*, 361–70.

Sen, S., Lam, S., Rashid, A., Cosley, D., Frankowski, D., Osterhouse, J. et al. (2006) Tagging, Communities, Vocabulary, Evolution. In *Proceedings of the 20th Anniversary Conference on Computer Supported Cooperative Work, Banff, Alberta, Canada*, 181–90.

Shardanand, U. and Maes, P. (1995) Social Information Filtering: algorithms for automating 'word of mouth'. In *Proceedings on Human Factors in Computing Systems*, 210–17.

Sherman, C. (2006) What's the Big Deal with Social Search?,
http://searchenginewatch.com/3623153.

Sinclair, J. and Cardew-Hall, M. (2008) The Folksonomy Tag Cloud: when is it useful?,
Journal of Information Science, **34** (1), 15–29.

Sinha, R. (2006) Findability with Tags: facets, clusters, and pivot browsing,
http://rashmisinha.com/2006/07/27/findability-with-tags-facets-clusters-and-pivot-browsing/.

Smith, M., Barash, V., Getoor, L. and Lauw, H. L. (2008) Leveraging Social Context for
Searching Social Media. In Soboroff, I., Agichtein, E. and Kumar, R. (eds),
*Proceedings of the 2008 ACM Workshop on Search in Social Media, Napa Valley,
California*, 91–4.

Stock, W. G. (2007a) *Information Retrieval: Informationen Suchen und Finden*, Oldenburg.

Stock, W. G. (2007b) Folksonomies and Science Communication: a mash-up of
professional science databases and Web 2.0 Services, *Information Services & Use*, **27**,
97–103.

Storey, M. A. D. (2007) Navigating Documents Using Ontologies, Taxonomies and
Folksonomies. In *Proceedings of the 2007 ACM Symposium on Document Engineering,
Winnipeg, Canada*, 2–2.

Sturtz, D. (2004) Communal Categorization: the folksonomy,
www.davidsturtz.com/drexel/622/sturtz-folksonomy.pdf.

Svensson, M. (1998) Social Navigation. In Dahlbäck, N. (ed.), *Exploring Navigation:
towards a framework for design and evaluation of navigation in electronic spaces.* SICS
Technical Report T98:01, Swedish Institute of Computer Science.

Szekely, B. and Torres, E. (2005) Ranking Bookmarks and Bistros: intelligent
community and folksonomy development,
http://torrez.us/archives/2005/07/13/tagrank.pdf.

Tonkin, E., Corrado, E. M., Moulaison, H. L., Kipp, M. E. I., Resmini, A., Pfeiffer, H. D.
et al. (2008) Collaborative and Social Tagging Networks, *Ariadne*, **54**,
www.ariadne.ac.uk/issue54/tonkin-et-al/.

Tredinnick, L. (2006) Web 2.0 and Business: a pointer to the intranets of the future?
Business Information Review, **23b** (4), 228–34.

Tudhope, D. and Nielsen, M. L. (2006) Introduction to Knowledge Organization
Systems and Services, *New Review of Hypermedia and Multimedia*, **12** (1), 3–9.

van Damme, C., Hepp, M. and Siorpaes, K. (2007) FolksOntology: an integrated
approach for turning folksonomies into ontologies. In *Proceedings of the European
Semantic Web Conference, Innsbruck, Austria*, 71–85.

van Hooland, S. (2006) From Spectator to Annotator: possibilities offered by user-
generated metadata for digital cultural heritage collections. In *Proceedings of the
CILIP Cataloguing and Indexing Group Annual Conference, Norwich, Great Britain*.

Vander Wal, T. (2004) Feed On This,
www.vanderwal.net/random/entrysel.php?blog=1562.

Vander Wal, T. (2005a) Folksonomy Explanations,
www.vanderwal.net/random/entrysel.php?blog=1622.

Vander Wal, T. (2005b) Explaining and Showing Broad and Narrow Folksonomies,
www.vanderwal.net/random/entrysel.php?blog=1635.

Viégas, F. and Wattenberg, M. (2008) Tag Clouds and the Case for Vernacular
Visualization, *Interactions*, **15** (4), 49–52.

Wang, J. and Davison, B. D. (2008) Explorations in Tag Suggestion and Query
Expansion. In Soboroff, I., Agichtein, E. and Kumar, R. (eds), *Proceedings of the
2008 ACM Workshop on Search in Social Media, Napa Valley, California*, 43–50.

Wash, R. and Rader, E. (2006) Collaborative Filtering with del.icio.us,
http://bierdoctor.com/papers/delicious_chi2006_wip_updated.pdf.

Wash, R. and Rader, E. (2007) Public Bookmarks and Private Benefits: an analysis of
incentives in social computing. In Grove, A. (ed.), *Joining Research and Practice:
social computing and information science: Proceedings of the 70th ASIS&T Annual
Meeting, Milwaukee, Wisconsin, USA* (CD-ROM).

Weinberger, D. (2005) Tagging and Why It Matters,
www.cyber.law.harvard.edu/home/uploads/507/07-WhyTaggingMatters.pdf.

Weinberger, K. Q., Slaney, M. and Van Zwol, R. (2008) Resolving Tag Ambiguity. In
*Proceedings of the 16th ACM International Conference on Multimedia, Vancouver,
Canada.*

Weiss, A. (2005) The Power of Collective Intelligence, *netWorker*, **9** (3), 16–23.

Wu, H., Zubair, M. and Maly, K. (2006) Harvesting Social Knowledge from
Folksonomies. In *Proceedings of the 17th Conference on Hypertext and Hypermedia,
Odense, Denmark*, 111–14.

Xu, Z., Fu, Y., Mao, J. and Su, D. (2006) Towards the Semantic Web: collaborative tag
suggestions, www.rawsugar.com/www2006/13.pdf.

Xue, G., Zeng, H., Chen, Z., Yu, Y., Ma, W. and Xi, W. et al. (2004) Optimizing Web
Search Using Click-through Data. In *Proceedings of the 13th ACM International
Conference on Information and Knowledge Management, Washington D. C., USA*, 118–
26.

Yanbe, Y., Jatowt, A., Nakamura, S. and Tanaka, K. (2007) Can Social Bookmarking
Enhance Search in the Web? In *Proceedings of the 7th ACM/IEEE Joint Conference on
Digital Libraries, Vancouver, BC, Canada*, 107–16.

Yin, D., Xue, Z., Hong, L. and Davison, B. D. (2010) A Probabilistic Model for
Personalized Tag Prediction. In *Proceedings of the 16th ACM SIGKDD International
Conference on Knowledge Discovery and Data Mining, Washington, USA*, 959–68.

Yoo, D. and Suh, Y. (2010) User-categorized Tags to Build a Structured Folksonomy. In
*Proceedings of the 2nd International Conference on Communication Software and
Networks, Singapore*, 160–4.

6

Digital information interaction as semantic navigation

Richard Kopak, Luanne Freund and Heather L. O'Brien

Introduction

In this chapter we focus on the research area of digital information interaction, which emphasizes searchers' direct engagement with and manipulation of information objects as they search and browse through digital information environments. This is an area of active research that has opened up in recent years as information retrieval (IR) research has expanded its focus from the mechanics of retrieval (i.e. indexing, data structures and retrieval algorithms) to include a broader 'retrieval in context' perspective that takes into account the whole system, the affective, cognitive and physical attributes of users and the environment in which searching takes place (Ingwersen and Järvelin, 2005). A number of meetings and workshops have focused on this area, including the Information Retrieval in Context (IRiX) workshops at the ACM SIGIR (Association for Computing Machinery Special Interest Group Information Retrieval) conference (2004–5), the Information Interaction in Context (IIiX) Conference (2006–ongoing) and the Human Computer Information Retrieval (HCIR) Workshops (2007–ongoing).

Immersive information systems, in which users are placed in content-rich environments with tools and technologies designed to help them search, filter and navigate through the information landscape, are now commonplace. In these types of environments, IR can no longer best be modelled as a transaction, but is more akin to an 'experience', in which searchers are influenced by the information objects they encounter and also shape and create their information environment by selecting, linking, tagging and commenting (Marchionini, 2008; Toms, 2002). For many people, these kinds of interactions with digital information are the primary means by which they read and learn, whether at work, at school or at leisure.

However, numerous studies that utilize server logs of bibliographic and web-based information systems have shown that digital information behaviour is markedly different from that in traditional print information environments. Digital information use tends to be non-linear, shallow and piecemeal. Readers jump frequently from one document to the next, 'skimming and bopping' through networked information spaces (JISC, 2008; Nicholas et al., 2007). Concerns have been raised that this type of information behaviour represents the 'intellectual equivalent of empty calories' (Rich, 2008) and inhibits deep, critical engagement with informational content (Marshall, 2005). How, then, can information systems be designed to support in-depth interaction with and use of a variety of information objects? How can IR systems and technologies be enhanced to provide better support for users as they read, learn and make sense of the world, and as they create and contribute new digital content themselves?

We frame our approach to these questions using the concept of semantic navigation. By semantic navigation, we mean that as people move through information, they actively construct meaning and make use of both explicit and implicit features of the information and its environment as guides in this process. This concept is based in part on Dillon's (2000) idea of spatial semantics. We suggest that one way to increase the quality and outcomes of information interaction is to design systems that provide better support for semantic navigation. This has implications for the design of IR interfaces and for exploratory search more generally.

The following section provides an explanation of the concept of semantic navigation, which draws upon perspectives from diverse fields: interactive IR, genre theory, studies of cognition, reading and hypertext, and user-experience design.

Semantic navigation

Our interest in the idea of semantic navigation was motivated largely by Dillon and Vaughan's (1997) argument that, in digital information environments, physical navigation metaphors are limited in their ability to fully support users' movement through what is otherwise a semantic, not a physical space. In invoking the concept of 'information shape', they suggest that a meaningful solution to users' navigational 'problems' will be achieved only when proper account is taken of the role that information itself plays in providing cues in aid of this navigation. Dillon and Vaughan further state that this is likely to occur only when the representation of meaning is in some way indicated in the navigational choices offered to users. Since navigation through information is essentially navigation through semantic space, it has as its purpose the 'endpoint of comprehension' (1997, 101), and thus directly involves movement through these representations of meaning.

From a psycholinguistic point of view, van Dijk and Kintsch (1983) note the importance of the role of 'global cohesion' in discourse comprehension and the importance of establishing inferencing bridges that connect informational components within and between texts. As a concern of semantic navigation, we might ask what representational cues can be provided that aid users in creating these bridging inferences. For example, what cues or signs based on the content or structural components of the content might help users to understand the informational purpose or meaning behind the creation of a link? Semantic navigation (or the idea of it) focuses our attention on how we can represent these meaning cues, signs and components at the interface itself.

The process of semantic navigation, like interactive search more generally, is strongly influenced by the context in which searcher, system and content interact. Two contexts are key among the many contextual factors at play: domain (areas of shared knowledge or practice) and task (activities undertaken to achieve goals). Domains are associated with shared epistemologies, patterns of communication and search behaviours, and directly affect the level at which a user is able to make inferences and meaningful connections between diverse ideas and concepts. Likewise, common types of tasks are associated with patterns in search behaviour and document selection. In particular, tasks establish criteria for determining the suitability and usefulness of information objects. Together, domain and task will influence semantic navigation by influencing the level and nature of understanding sought, the types of information that are recognized and valued, and the information-gathering strategies employed.

Supporting semantic navigation

The next step is to consider how we can provide support for this process within information systems. We envision at least three broad approaches. The first is to expose to users the cues and meanings that are latent in information objects and in the environment, for example, through labelling, highlighting and mapping. By exposing the semantic scaffolding in this way, information systems will provide users with a better opportunity to understand the big picture and to move sure-footedly through the environment. The second approach is to provide users with tools and markers that they can use to probe the environment and to document their own understanding as they journey through it. Providing users with a means to interact fully with their environment allows them to make the shift from passive to active learners and to more critically engage with the content. Thirdly, the design of information environments should shape the overall user experience. The content and its representation should be interesting, relevant and appealing so that users will be motivated and drawn in, and the technology should be intuitive so that the tools do not get in the way of the work at hand.

In the sections to follow, we introduce a number of more specific research areas that have the potential to contribute to semantic navigation: genre, linking, annotation and user engagement. Each of these represents a possible avenue for innovative IR research.

Document genre

Most information objects in digital collections are artefacts of human communication and thus tend to be characterized by genre: recognizable patterns of communication based on commonalities of purpose, form and content, arising from a particular context (Yates and Orlikowski, 1992). FAQs, blogs and home pages are common web genres, but an array of more traditional genres also exist in digital collections: reports, reviews, journal articles and books are a few examples. Document genres serve as cues for readers to indicate when and why a document was created and by whom, how it is intended to be used, the likely structure and arrangement of content, and sometimes even the nature of the message contained therein.

Current genre research extends across many disciplines: creative and technical writing, linguistics, organizational behaviour and information systems, to name a few. A common thread in this research is a focus on the rhetorical and functional role of documents, which complements the more traditional topical approach to document analysis and classification. Accordingly, genre recognition primes the reader to interpret a text in the framework of its role within the sphere of human social activity (Bazerman, Little and Chavkin, 2003).

Studies in organizational settings have shown that, over time, distinctive repertoires of genres establish themselves in response to local needs and situations. Spinuzzi (2003) refers to these repertoires as genre ecologies, emphasizing their situated, organic and dynamic nature. Developing within these ecologies are genre systems, which are small sets of functionally linked genres, such as an order form, an invoice and a shipping notice. Mapping out these genre ecologies in the form of hierarchical or faceted classification systems is a common approach to studying genre; however, the complexity and variability of genre use continues to challenge researchers seeking to develop standard approaches (Crowston, Kwaśnik and Rubleske, 2011).

The role of genre in semantic navigation

A genre-based approach to information interaction has the potential to support semantic navigation in several ways. First, genre serves as an indicator of the purpose or intended function of information objects and can therefore help to guide inter-object navigation and document selection. For example, searchers in workplace settings may actively search for specific genres (e.g. reports, memos, manuals) that they expect to be suited to particular tasks. Searchers also use genre to make decisions about which documents to select from a search engine results page, depending on their intended use of the information. Second, genre raises expectations as to the internal structure of an information object and its component parts. Knowledge of this structure facilitates intra-object navigation and information extraction and provides a searcher with a 'mental framework into which she can put incoming data, providing context and cues for comprehension' (Dillon, 2008). For example, readers familiar with how-to guides know that they are likely to contain lists of step-by-step instructions, and may choose to skip directly to that section when trying to extract information quickly. Third, because genre tends to be expressed visually, in the shape of a document and its salient structural elements, such as headings and blocks of text, searchers often are able to identify genres quickly as they move through digital information environments, which helps them to make sense of those environments, supports selection and navigation decisions, and facilitates reading and learning.

Despite the prevalence of genres and the important role they play in human information interaction, the concept of genre has received relatively little attention in the design of IR systems. One of the reasons for this is the familiar 'bag of words' approach to text representation, which assumes that most of the meaning in texts exists at the token level. A small number of experimental systems have incorporated genre either explicitly in the display of search results or implicitly in the matching and ranking algorithms. For example, the Easify system was an early attempt to cluster web search results by subject and by genre (Bretan et al., 1998) and the X-Site system used the relationships between genres and tasks to influence the ranking of search results (Yeung, Freund and Clarke, 2007). The recent growth in popularity of faceted search systems has resulted in greater use of genre as a means of filtering search results. One prominent example is the UK Parliament website, which enables users to limit and narrow search results by content type, e.g. business papers, debates, legislation.

Characteristic of these approaches to designing genre-enabled search systems is the focus on the input-output (query-results) paradigm, which represents only a small portion of information interaction activities in digital environments. The design of genre-enabled systems to support semantic navigation will require that we extend our thinking to examine the role that genre can play in exploratory, interactive and immersive information systems.

Areas for future research: genre

Genre research is both fascinating and challenging because genres are expressive of the complex and many-layered nuances of human communication. In any given information environment there may be hundreds or thousands of different categories and subcategories of genres that are recognized more or less consistently within user communities. We know that genres carry meaning to readers, but we still do not know how best to make use of this in information systems design.

Genre classification represents a major research challenge. There is a need to identify robust, standardized genre taxonomies for the world wide web and for specific domains, including education, research, government and commerce. This will require decisions as to scope and granularity. How many genres should be included and how specific should the categories be? Researchers have already made progress towards identifying feature sets and methods suited to the automatic classification of genres, and early results are promising (Santini, 2008); however, much of this work has been done using formal test collections, rather than live collections of digital documents. How well these automatic methods will work in the real world remains an open question.

Genre representation is another area for future research. We know that readers are adept at recognizing genres when they see whole documents, but can labels, summaries or visual representations of documents serve the same purpose? How can interfaces for searching and browsing support genre recognition and use?

Apart from these challenges, a broader question remains: how can genre be used to structure information environments for browsing and learning? The natural groupings and relationships within genre repertoires seem to offer potential for defining dynamic functional browsing spaces that would support the establishment of global cohesion in the comprehension of digital information. Further work is needed on genre in combination with other approaches to semantic navigation, in order to explore this potential.

Annotation

Annotation of documents has a long record in the history of written communication. As far back as the 5th century BC, scholia, i.e. critical or explanatory text, were used as marginal commentary to add value in some way to the text as presented. Since that time, annotation has maintained much of its inherent capability to 'comment' upon existing work, but has become much more pervasive as a form of personal commentary, as opposed to its more historic role as scholarly interpretation in, for example, a critical edition. In modern, digital environments, annotation might be described as a more generalized, communicative process that not only adds value to content for one's own individual purposes but increasingly may also act to supply cues to other users in their encounters with the same information.

Although annotation has different meanings in different contexts, for our purposes in this chapter we define it as the permanent and semi-permanent marks, words and notes that a user makes around content while engaged with that content. For example, while reading a document, someone may underline a sentence, doodle in the margin or write a more elaborate note commenting on the content of the document. The particular individual motivations for making annotations such as these are varied, but there is evidence to suggest that annotations serve a common set of purposes. Marshall (1998, 2010), for example, outlines six different functions that annotation can fulfil, including 'signal for future attention' and 'interpretation'. She also enumerates a series of 'forms' associated with these different functions, e.g. a reader may place a tick/checkmark or asterisk in the margin (form) to signal or draw attention to this passage for later use (function).

In many ways, annotation provides an important opportunity for users to capture and save the 'intellectual capital' they create in the normal course of interacting with information. It does so in a very efficient way as well, because the annotation is ordinarily made at the point of closest encounter with the information and is recorded in proximity to it. This has significance because it acts to describe and draw attention to an interesting or relevant segment in a document (for oneself and others) and, if the annotation is in the form of a longer note, it may provide key descriptive terms for the associated content.

The role of annotation in semantic navigation

An essential aspect of semantic navigation is the use of content and associated contextual and structural information, e.g. meaning representations, and genre to provide cues to users in order to support their navigational choices. Important in providing information-based cues for the purpose of navigation is the provision of a means for readers to become further engaged in the processing of the information while reading, including the ability to leave traces of their intellectual activities while engaging with the content. One way of achieving this is to facilitate a closer coupling between the reading and writing process (Brown and Brown, 2004). After all, we often read in order to write, and in paper-based systems it is commonplace to make marginal notations and underline phrases or sentences in our books and journals. Closer integration of these activities enables more 'active reading'. Personal annotation has been long recognized as a fundamental component of a more active reading strategy (Adler, 1940) because it promotes 'thinking, and thinking tends to express itself in words, spoken or written'. O'Hara et al. (1998) studied undergraduate students' use of library documents and found that writing and reading were 'inextricably intertwined'. In many environments, the act of commenting on existing documentation through annotations is the primary form of writing (Brush et al., 2001).

In electronic systems, enabling readers to express thoughts in written form through annotation not only provides for deeper engagement with the content but has implications for IR. Annotations enable readers to contribute additional information that can be used for retrieving or 'refinding' (Blandford and Attfield, 2010) specific information for their own personal future use. Furthermore, Schilit, Golovchinsky and Price (1998) noted the saliency of annotation in visual search and the affordance it provides not only in flagging content for future use but in providing a short descriptive or interpretive synopsis to quickly remind the reader of the topic, purpose or interpretation of the related content. In this way, the descriptive terms added to content through the natural course of engaging with the ideas may serve as a form of tagging. These 'tags' could be harvested and indexed as descriptive metadata. Furthermore, if displayed in a convenient way, e.g. a tag cloud, they could be used to collocate and provide quick access to all instances of the 'tag' in individual documents or in a collection of documents employed for the current information task.

From a social informatics point of view, descriptive annotations of this kind may be used by others to locate information within a document that they are encountering for the first time. It is possible, for example, to have public tag clouds comprising the terms identified in all annotations made on a particular document: tags that are not 'attributed' but that occur as a by-product of the 'basic and often unselfconscious way in which readers interact with texts' (Marshall, 2010).

Areas for future research: annotation

A growing number of annotation tools are available for use in digital reading environments, reflecting a demand for applications that enable the kind of interaction focused on in this chapter. Chiang (2010), for example, enumerated over 20 different annotation applications that are available for highlighting and making notes while reading. These tools continue to be created, but often in the absence of underlying principles for design that are founded on research-based annotation behaviours. For example, Marshall's (1998, 2010; see also Chiang, 2010) work has been mentioned on several occasions as one of the few streams of research that has tried to map the motivations or functions of annotation onto the particular forms (i.e. tools) that best enable these functions to be carried out.

Further empirical work is needed in this area.

For many years, IR has been primarily focused on the retrieval of objects and not on direct interaction with them, and the role of information interaction in retrieval has not been closely studied. The major questions to be pursued here involve how we can best take advantage of the human capital invested in the creation of annotations. For example, can our understanding of genre and the rhetorical conventions it reflects be used to suggest standard sets of terms that reflect the kind of information that is likely to be found in a particular section of, say, a scholarly journal article? Will annotations, and the words that comprise them, have different meanings, depending on the particular document component, e.g. the 'Introduction', in which they occur? Are there automated processes that can parse the annotations and reflect variations in the 'meaning' of the terms, based on their position in the document?

Of increasing interest are questions concerning the value of annotations in social or collaborative environments. How, for example, do we decide which annotations in a shared annotation space are most valuable for a specific purpose that we might have while reading a document? In other words, how might we distinguish between annotations that provide 'good' additional content and 'not so good' content, or content that is most appropriate for our needs? Are there additional social markers that need to be included in annotations to signal the level of 'cognitive authority' that the annotation has, based on its authorship? Equally important are interface design issues concerning the manner in which annotation threads, written by multiple users, can be best ordered and displayed within the confines of a typical display.

Linking

Links, in modern information systems, are important and are more than a vestige of arcane hypertext systems from days gone by. The world wide web, the largest and most popular information system of our time, is a rudimentary form of hypertext and is highly dependent on links to provide navigation. Yet, the IR literature, in many ways, continues to view the information object as primary. While the hypertext structure of the web is used to assess document relevance in web IR, links themselves tend to be treated as neutral, rather than functional or meaningful, connectives. In the early years of the web, Burbules (1998) noted, somewhat ironically, that links' 'ease of use makes them seem merely shortcuts, and subservient to the important things: the information sources that they make available. Their speed in taking a user from one point to another makes the moment of transition too fleeting to merit reflection; the link-event becomes invisible' (1998, 104).

Given the central role of linking, especially in web-based information environments, there is value in exploring ways to make more evident a link's innate capacity to carry meaning. As opposed to the passive action of following a link, the act of creating a link between two pieces of information causes readers to create (or to become conscious of) the underlying semantic relationships between information objects. Links represent the connections between ideas and act as bridges to navigate the meanings shared. Hence, it is important to offer readers (now as authors) the means to easily instantiate links during the act of reading. Users require tools that will transform them from passive users of links to active, engaged creators of them.

The role of linking in semantic navigation

If we accept the importance of the link as an opportunity to create meaningful informational relationships, and further accept that perhaps its capacity is underused, the question arises as to what qualities links have that would allow them to be better used. One possible answer involves the ability of the link to indicate or convey information about aspects of the relationship between information objects in advance of traversing the link; in short, a form of link typing. Landow (1997) first suggested this as advantageous in hypertextual environments because typing a link can usefully limit its interpretation to a specific kind of relationship (e.g. 'defines', or 'exemplifies') that indicates connectedness on semantic or rhetorical grounds. When clearly labelled, typed links also provide a kind of preview that aids in navigation, i.e. it helps to answer questions like 'do I really want to see a "definition" right now?' and aids in guiding users to follow those links leading to information that most closely matches the kind of information needed at that point in the search process. In this way, links and the relationships they represent can be viewed from the perspective of function, in addition to their more frequent use as indicating topic.

From this perspective, we can help people in navigating information semantically by enabling them to capture and make explicit the nature of the relationship between nodes of information. Link typing based on functional categories (Kopak, 1999, 2000), for example, enables users to name links based on purpose, e.g. A defines B, C illustrates D, E summarizes F. Kopak and Chiang (2007) report the results of a study of a prototype journal-reading system where users created persistent links between content elements in multiple journal articles and then typed the link relationship from a fixed set of terms describing these functional relationships. As a result, readers become authors by creating functionally meaningful relationships between these fragments of text. Movement through the articles within the system can later be recalled and retraced with navigation guided by the purpose and role of the associated information in facilitating comprehension.

From the reader's perspective, typed linked relationships (as a visible part of an electronic document, e.g. a mouseover, tooltip, etc.) have the advantage of priming the transition from one information object to the next and increasing the cognitive 'visibility' of the link relationship. Specification of these functional relationships increases the level of coherence (van Dijk and Kintsch, 1983; Lorch and Lorch, 1995) between the objects being connected and provides 'scent' (Pirolli, 2007) that users can follow to more useful information, given the particular information task at hand. When this is combined with annotation, the reader can amend or supplement the instantiated link type with additional descriptive link relationships or further commentary.

Areas for future research: linking

Although the idea of enabling users to easily create their own links through the normal course of interacting with information seems appealing, there is a shortage of research-based evidence to suggest how it might best be accomplished. In Kopak and Chiang's (2007) study, users of a prototype annotation and linking system had difficulty, in the cognitive sense, in knowing when and how to actively create links between content segments within the set of journal articles provided to them. It appeared that while most everyone had a clear idea of how to 'use' links, they did not have a sufficient 'mental model' of how and when to instantiate the connections they were making at the cognitive level.

Further research that would lead to more robust link typologies that reflect the specific nature of not only the domain but also the task motivating the information use is also required. A number of general link typologies have been developed over the years (Trigg, 1983; Parunak, 1991; Baron, Tague-Sutcliffe and Kinnucan 1996; Kopak, 2000), but none has adequately mapped the relationship between task and domain. Buckingham Shum et al. (2007) provide an example of how 'discourse ontologies' can be utilized in argumentation systems for specific communities of interest.

The idea of socially created hypertexts is also an interesting direction for future research. As with annotation, there is a significant opportunity to capture the intellectual capital already invested in the creation of links on an individual basis. For example, individual scholars could create series of links (that might also be typed) for their own use in writing a scholarly paper that enabled them to retrace the paths and connections discovered in their earlier explorations of the material. All or some of these might be shared to a public space. The important question then becomes how to determine which links are chosen and aggregated from among all contributed links. Scalability is an issue in this regard, as not all links can usefully be shown. What is required is a means to automatically arbitrate the selection process so that only those 'high quality' or 'high frequency' links are shown.

User engagement

In *Computers as Theatre*, Brenda Laurel challenged the traditional view of IR as 'looking for something to examining or experiencing something' (1993, 140). She argued that attention should be paid to the intellectual and affective activities of 'perceiving, interpreting and experiencing information' (1993, 140). Since that time, user experience (UX) has emerged as a prevalent theme in human–computer interaction research and design. UX is defined as 'a person's perceptions and responses that result from the use or anticipated use of a product, system or service' (ISO, 2008). A focus on UX pushes us to think beyond usability to design interactions that are fun, fulfilling, aesthetic, interactive and engaging.

One of the characteristics of UX research and design is an emphasis on a holistic approach to human interaction with technology. The user's experience has been characterized as a sense-making process where individual actions and reactions combine to form memorable experiences that may be reflected upon and communicated to others. McCarthy and Wright (2004) propose that this unfolding of experience is comprised of 'threads': compositional, spatio-temporal, sensual and emotional. The compositional thread is the narrative of the experience, while the spatio-temporal thread situates UX in a specific time and physical/virtual space. The emotional and sensual threads emphasize the importance of cognition, emotion and physicality in interactions with technology, e.g. the ability to perceive information through touch, sight and sound.

Key to UX is engagement: the quality of being drawn in, captivated by and actively participating in an interaction. O'Brien and Toms (2010) isolated six attributes of engagement: aesthetic appeal, novelty, focused attention, felt involvement, perceived usability and endurability, i.e. the user's overall evaluation of the experience as successful, worthwhile etc. Engaging user experiences have been studied in numerous contexts, such as hypertext, video games, museums and educational multimedia systems; information searching and browsing environments have been investigated to a lesser degree (O'Brien and Toms, 2008). However, research conducted in different disciplines and across different systems suggests that engaging systems share some commonalities. First, they have the ability to attract and maintain the interest of users by providing them with continuous feedback, appropriate levels of challenge and control over the interaction. Second, engaging technologies stimulate exploration and enjoyment by embedding interactive and multimedia features (e.g. video, audio, graphics) in the navigation and presentation of information (O'Brien and Toms, 2008).

The role of engagement in semantic navigation

Attention to user engagement has the potential to support semantic navigation by enriching the user's experiences with the system and the content. An engaging information environment allows users to manipulate information tools and objects in a direct and intuitive manner, provides awareness of the task environment and the information objects it contains and supports the user in carrying out different tasks (Liew, Foo and Chennupati, 2001). In other words, experiential information environments embody malleability, adaptability and connectivity. Engaging information systems facilitate the users' affective responses (e.g. meaning making) and cognitive processes (e.g. learning, decision making) by enabling them to move in a purposeful manner through an interactive, content-rich environment.

When we consider users' experiences in interactive information environments, it is useful to articulate different types of engagement. In the context of digital reading, Mangen discusses involvement with 'the fictional world' of a story (i.e. phenomenological immersion) and the tools delivering the story (i.e. technological immersion) (2008, 406). We might think about this distinction more generally outside the context of reading by recognizing that users become engaged with textual and multimedia content and with tools, e.g. features, appearance or capabilities of the technology. Semantic navigation uses tools (e.g. links, annotations) and content cues (e.g. genre) to support deep engagement with content. In these environments, users are able to actively construct meaning, make connections to their prior knowledge and other content they have examined, or satisfy an instrumental need for information through browsing, searching and processing information.

To support content engagement in IR systems, we need to provide 'cues' in results pages and documents that enable searchers to quickly assess the salience of information and 'dive into' the text. We must also consider how to make these cues relevant to individual users. Currently, commercial search engines are moving in this direction by emphasizing diversity in search results: for every query, a range of search results are presented, categorized by choice of format (video, images) and genre (news, blogs, reference materials) so as to facilitate selection of the most promising source. One of the keys to engagement is allowing users to choose what they wish to engage with. This means personalizing the interface so as to enable users to display the features that they find most pleasing or functional in a particular setting and permit them to 'turn off' distracting or unnecessary features (Hillesund, 2010).

Areas for future research: user engagement

Focusing on semantic navigation of information spaces promotes a more holistic examination of users' paths and the ways in which their decisions alter their affective and cognitive goals, conceptions of tasks and content and evaluations of outcomes with information systems. In addition to looking at the ways in which a single interaction with a technology unfolds, it is necessary to consider how these episodes build over time to form larger experiences and how people's relationships, familiarity and emotional response to the technology change over time (McCarthy and Wright, 2004). As such, more longitudinal studies are needed to examine the long-term adoption and use of immersive information systems. Focusing on user engagement creates measurement challenges. Standard usability metrics of efficiency and effectiveness are not sufficient for assessing affective and cognitive changes in users that form the trajectory of experience. Instead, we must examine ways in which to capture the dynamics of UX through a combination of quantitative and qualitative methods, such as observation, questionnaires, biometrics, eye tracking and interviews, and look at ways in which we can make sense of and triangulate mixed-methods approaches. What makes an 'engaging' information-interaction experience? How do we develop metrics that capture the dynamics, temporality and richness of experience?

Another area that merits further examination is the materiality of information interaction. The range of computer devices is growing, as are the numbers of users who own such products. E-book readers, iPhones and other small-scale devices require new ways of interacting physically – through sound, for example – and promote interaction in different contexts. How are such devices changing the locations and modalities in which we interact with information and how can we support semantic navigation on a range of devices in unknown contexts? In addition, what should these interfaces look like? How do we develop guidelines for the design of information-interaction devices that will promote engaging user experiences?

Conclusion

From our perspective, the purpose of IR is not simply to locate relevant information objects, but to engage in active, purposeful learning: to read, to become informed, to make connections, to evaluate, to carry out tasks and, in the process, to contribute back to the information environment. The concept of semantic navigation offers an innovative perspective on IR that places greater emphasis on engagement with and use of digital information in the context of real-world tasks and activities. In this way, it complements and extends current research on exploratory search.

At the outset of this chapter we asked how search systems could enable this type of information interaction. Drawing upon the various approaches to semantic navigation presented here, we can begin to envision an answer to this question. In the broadest sense, search systems can no longer afford to consider the process of retrieving information as separate from its use, as the two are inextricably linked through the user's experience. Systems need to take into account the breadth of the user's experience with information, from searching to reading and writing, as well as the multiple dimensions of that experience: intellectual, emotional and spatio-temporal. In order to motivate and engage users in information interaction, systems should employ a range of techniques, such as narrative, visual and spatial metaphors and direct interaction, and embrace principles such as novelty, diversity and challenge, in addition to relevance and usefulness.

Such systems should afford users the opportunity to understand not only what the content is about, but also what they can do with it. Structural, navigational and functional cues in the form of genre labels and typed links could be embedded in the environment to help users recognize and use information objects and understand the relationships between them. The provision of annotation and linking tools at the point of encountering information, to allow for users to leave their own markers in the environment and to document their intellectual and navigational paths, would also support a richer interaction with the content.

The logical progression of this approach is to tie these local and individualistic approaches to semantic navigation into a broader social conception of shared and communally constructed semantic infrastructures within digital information environments. In this vision, the traces left behind by users interacting with information will enrich the content for others and serve as input for systems to learn and evolve over time.

References

Adler, M. (1940) How to Mark a Book, *Saturday Review of Literature*, 6 July, 11–12.

Baron, L., Tague-Sutcliffe, J. and Kinnucan, M. (1996) Labeled, Typed Links as Cues when Reading Hypertext Documents, *Journal of the American Association for Information Science*, **47** (12), 896–908.

Bazerman, C., Little, J. and Chavkin, T. (2003) The Production of Information for Genred Activity Spaces, *Written Communication*, **20** (4), 455–77.

Blandford, A. and Attfield, S. (2010) *Interacting with Information*, Morgan and Claypool.

Bretan, I. et al. (1998) Web-specific Genre Visualization. In Maurer, H. A. and Olson, R. G. (eds), *Proceedings of WebNet held on 7–12 November 1998, Orlando, Florida, USA,* AACE.

Brown, P. J. and Brown, H. (2004) Integrating Reading and Writing of Documents, *Journal of Digital Information,* **5** (1), http://journals.tdl.org/jodi/article/view/72/118.

Brush, A. J., Bargeron, D., Gupta, A. and Cadiz, J. J. (2001) Robust Annotation Positioning in Digital Documents. In *Proceedings of SIGCHI 200 held on 31 March – 5 April 2001, Seattle, WA, USA,* Association for Computing Machinery.

Buckingham Shum, S., Uren, V., Li, G., Sereno, B. and Mancini, C. (2007) Modeling Naturalistic Argumentation in Research Literatures: representation and interaction design issues, *International Journal of Intelligent Systems,* **22**, 17–47.

Burbules, N. (1998) Rhetorics of the Web: hyperreading and critical literacy. In Snyder, I. (ed.), *Page to Screen: taking literacy into the electronic era,* Routledge.

Chiang, C. (2010) *A Multi-Dimensional Approach to the Study of Online Annotation,* unpublished doctoral dissertation, University of British Columbia.

Crowston, K., Kwasnik, B., and Rubleske, J. (2011) Problems in the Use-centered Development of a Taxonomy of Web Genres. In Mehler, A., Sharoff, S. and Santini, M., (eds) *Genres on the Web: computational Models and Empirical Studies.* Text, Speech and Language Technology, vol. 42, part 2, Springer, 69–84, DOI: 10.1007/978-90-481-9178-9_4.

Dillon, A. (2000) Spatial Semantics: how users derive shape from information space, *Journal of the American Society for Information Science and Technology,* **51** (6), 521–8.

Dillon, A. (2008) Bringing Genre into Focus: why information has shape, *The Bulletin of the American Society for Information Science and Technology,* **34** (5), 17–19.

Dillon, A. and Vaughan, M. (1997) 'It's the Journey and the Destination': shape and the emergent property of genre in evaluating digital documents, *New Review of Multimedia and Hypermedia,* **3**, 91–106.

Hillesund, T. (2010) Digital Reading Spaces: how expert readers handle books, the web and electronic paper, *First Monday,* **15** (4–5), http://firstmonday.org/htbin/cgiwrap/bin/ojs/index.php/fm/article/view/27 62/2504.

Ingwersen, P. and Järvelin, K. (2005) *The Turn: integration of information seeking and retrieval in context,* vol. 18, Springer.

ISO DIS 9241-210 (2008) *Ergonomics of Human System Interaction – Part 210: Human-centred design for interactive systems (formerly known as 13407),* International Standards Organization.

JISC (2008) *Information Behaviour of the Researcher of the Future,* www.bl.uk/news/pdf/googlegen.pdf.

Kopak, R. W. (1999) Functional Link Typing in Hypertext, *ACM Computing Surveys,* **31** (4), 16–22.

Kopak, R. W. (2000) *A Taxonomy of Link Types for Use in Hypertext*, unpublished doctoral dissertation, Faculty of Information Studies, University of Toronto.

Kopak, R. W. and Chiang, C. N. (2007) Annotating and Linking in the Open Journal Systems, *First Monday*, **12** (10), http://firstmonday.org/htbin/cgiwrap/bin/ojs/index.php/fm/article/view/1961/1838.

Landow, G. P. (1997) *Hypertext 2.0: the convergence of contemporary critical theory and technology*, Johns Hopkins University Press.

Laurel, B. (1993) *Computers as Theatre*, Addison-Wesley.

Liew, C. L., Foo, S. and Chennupati, K. R. (2001) A Proposed Integrated Environment for Enhanced User Interaction and Value-adding of Electronic Documents: an empirical evaluation, *Journal of the American Society for Information Science and Technology*, **52** (1), 22–35.

Lorch, R. F. and Lorch, E. P. (1995) Effects of Organizational Signals on Text-processing Strategies, *Journal of Educational Psychology*, **87** (4), 537–44.

Mangen, A. (2008) Hypertext Fiction Reading: haptics and immersion, *Journal of Research in Reading*, **31** (4), 404–19.

Marchionini, G. (2008) Human-information Interaction Research and Development, *Library and Information Science Research*, **30** (3), 165–74.

Marshall, C. C. (1998) Toward an Ecology of Hypertext Annotation. In *Proceedings of 9th ACM Conference on Hypertext and Hypermedia: links, objects, time and space-structure in hypermedia systems*, 40–9.

Marshall, C. C. (2005) Reading and Interactivity in the Digital Library: creating an experience that transcends paper. In Marcum, D. B. and George, G. (eds) *Digital Library Development: the view from Kanazawa*, Libraries Unlimited, 127–45.

Marshall, C. C. (2010) *Reading and Writing the Electronic Book*, Morgan & Claypool.

McCarthy, J. and Wright, P. C. (2004) *Technology as Experience*, MIT Press.

Nicholas, D., Huntington, P., Jamali, H. R. and Dobrowolski, T. (2007) Characterising and Evaluating Information Seeking Behaviour in a Digital Environment: spotlight on the 'bouncer', *Information Processing and Management*, **43** (4), 1085–102.

O'Brien, H. L. and Toms, E. G. (2008) What is User Engagement? A conceptual framework for defining user engagement with technology, *Journal of the American Society for Information Science and Technology*, **59** (6), 938–55.

O'Brien, H. L. and Toms, E. G. (2010) The Development and Evaluation of a Survey to Measure User Engagement in E-commerce Environments, *Journal of the American Society for Information Science and Technology*, **61** (1), 50–69.

O'Hara, K., Smith, F., Newman, W. and Sellen, A. (1998) Student Readers' Use of Library Documents: implications for library technologies. In *Proceedings of CHI 1998 Human Factors in Computing Systems*, 233–40.

Parunak, H. V. (1991) Ordering the Information Graph. In Berk, E. and Devlin, J. (eds), *Hypertext/Hypermedia Handbook*, McGraw-Hill Publishing Co., Inc., 299–325.

Pirolli, P. (2007) *Information Foraging: adaptive interaction with information*, Oxford University Press.

Rich, M. (2008) Literacy Debate: online, R U really reading?, *New York Times*, 27 July, www.nytimes.com/2008/07/27/books/27reading.html.

Santini, M. (2008) Zero, Single, or Multi? Genre of web pages through the users' perspective, *Information Processing and Management*, **44** (2), 702–37.

Schilit, B. N., Golovchinsky, G. and Price, M. N. (1998) Beyond Paper: supporting active reading with free form Digital Ink annotations. In *Proceedings of CHI 1998, Los Angeles, CA*, 249–56.

Spinuzzi, C. (2003) *Tracing Genres through Organizations: a sociocultural approach to information design*, MIT Press.

Toms, E. G. (2002) Information Interaction: providing a framework for information architecture, *Journal of the American Society for Information Science and Technology*, **53** (10), 855–62.

Trigg, R. H. (1983) *A Network-Based Approach to Text Handling for the Online Scientific Community*, unpublished doctoral dissertation, University of Maryland, College Park.

van Dijk, T. A. and Kintsch, W. (1983) *Strategies of Discourse Comprehension*, Academic Press.

Yates, J. and Orlikowski, W. J. (1992) Genres of Organizational Communication: a structurational approach to studying communication and media, *Academy of Management Review*, **17** (2), 299–326.

Yeung, P. C. K., Freund, L. and Clarke, C. L. A. (2007) X-Site: a workplace search tool for software engineers. In *Proceedings of the 30th Annual International ACM SIGIR Conference held 23–27 July 2007, Amsterdam*, Association for Computing Machinery.

7

Assessing web search engines: a webometric approach

Mike Thelwall

Introduction

Information Retrieval (IR) research typically evaluates search systems in terms of the standard precision, recall and F-measures to weight the relative importance of precision and recall (e.g. van Rijsbergen, 1979). All of these assess the extent to which the system returns good matches for a query. In contrast, webometric measures are designed specifically for web search engines and are designed to monitor changes in results over time and various aspects of the internal logic of the way in which search engine select the results to be returned. This chapter introduces a range of webometric measurements and illustrates them with case studies of Google, Bing and Yahoo! This is a very fertile area for simple and complex new investigations into search engine results.

The modern commercial web search engine is a highly complex system (Arasu et al., 2001) with vast social and commercial significance (Van Couvering, 2004, 2007). Although they can be evaluated to some extent with traditional IR measures like precision and recall, web search engines behave differently from traditional IR systems in many respects. Three key differences are the importance of rank order in the results; the limitation to 1,000 matches per query; and the goal of delivering relevant and useful results rather than technically accurate matches (in the sense of: Bar-Ilan and Peritz, 2008). In response, evaluation metrics have been developed to measure new characteristics of web search engines, such as the effectiveness of the rank order of the results (Zaragoza, Cambazoglu and Baeza-Yates, 2010), mean average precision (Turpin and Scholer, 2006) and discounted cumulative gain (Järvelin and Kekalainen, 2002). A broad common goal is to assess the extent to which any web search engine delivers good and relevant results to users. For some information scientists, however, IR goals are not sufficient with regard to web search engines, for two reasons.

First, search engines like Google are so important in academia and daily life that it is important for information professionals to understand something of how they work and what their limitations are. Second, web search engines are used in research as a way of accessing relevant web data, particularly in the fields of webometrics (Bar-Ilan, 2004; Thelwall, Vaughan and Björneborn, 2005) and computational linguistics (Kilgarriff and Grefenstette, 2003; Meyer et al., 2003). These applications are often for purposes that completely ignore all the URLs returned and just use the hit count estimates (HCEs; see below) or superficially parse the URLs and associated information. In this context non-standard questions can be critical, such as the extent to which the results change over time and the relationship between reported HCEs and the number of URLs returned for a query. In response to these new needs, metrics such as HCE error rate (Uyar, 2009b) have been designed by webometricians and applied to major web search engines (for a range of definitions see Bar-Ilan, 2002).

One prominent type of webometric investigation has been the analysis of search engine coverage of the web to answer questions like: how big is the web? what fraction of the web does a search engine cover? and how much overlap is there in the coverage of search engines? In the early years of the web some academics produced estimates of the proportion of the web indexed by search engines (Bharat and Broder, 1998; Ding and Marchionini, 1996; Lawrence and Giles, 1998, 1999). However, these estimates are no longer possible, for technical reasons (Thelwall, 2002). It also no longer makes sense to talk about the size of the web because many of the largest and most popular websites, such as Google and Facebook, are mostly used for pages that are created on demand in response to user requests. For example, when a Google query is submitted it builds a new web page to report the results. Hence the notion of 'the number of pages in google.com' is not valid. More generally, part of the web that is difficult or impossible for search engines to index is sometimes known as the invisible or dark web and there have been some attempts to estimate the size of parts of it (Lewandowski and Mayr, 2006). Figure 7.1 (overleaf) illustrates in general terms the sources of differences between the web and the results that a search engine returns, with the (false) assumption that there is such a thing as 'all web pages'.

The remainder of this chapter falls into three separate categories: longitudinal studies of changes in results over time; internal consistency investigations of the differences between the results apparently known by a search engine and those it reports; and experiments into search engine coverage bias.

Temporal changes

Longitudinal studies of search engines began when web researchers noticed that the results for a query varied over time and it was even possible for the

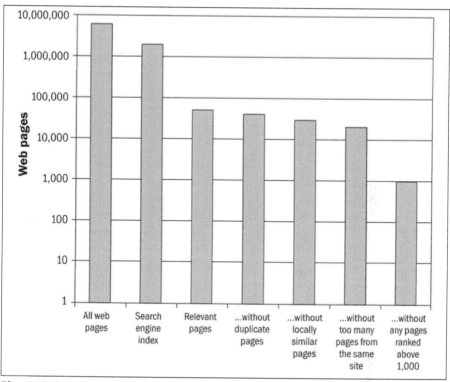

Figure 7.1 *Factors influencing the number of results returned for a search (hypothetical figures, but note the logarithmic scale) (Thelwall, 2008b)*

same query to return a dramatically different HCEs from one instant to the next. Note that the HCE is the estimated number of search matches reported, typically at the top of the results page (e.g. the 10,000 in 'Results 1–10 of about 10,000' in Google). In response, several investigations have tracked a set of queries over a period of time, graphing fluctuations in the results.

The metrics used tend to be very simple: either the estimated or actual number of results returned for a query or the presence or absence of a particular URL in a set of search results. Studies typically report averages over a large set of queries to reveal general patterns. The remainder of this section summarizes the results of this kind of study, mentioning techniques when appropriate.

Early research confirmed that search engine HCEs fluctuated wildly over time in the late 1990s (Bar-Ilan, 1999; Rousseau, 1999). The reason for this seemed to be that search engine indexes were internally split into separate parts and the HCEs were obtained by extrapolating from the results of the fraction searched (Badue et al., in press; Barroso, Dean, and Holzle, 2003). Hence, if a fraction of 1% of the whole index was searched and 45 results were found, then the HCE would be 45 × 100 = 4500. If the matches were unevenly split amongst the index fractions, then this would cause errors and potential fluctuations in the results. A consequence of such fluctuations was a recommendation that those using HCEs in research should use several identical queries and use the average of the HCEs (Rousseau, 1999). At the turn of the millennium, HCEs seemed to become much more consistent, although there does not seem to have been a public explanation about why this should be so. Longitudinal studies started to reveal a very different pattern: consistent results over long periods of time, with occasional sharp jumps. An explanation for this new behaviour was provided by research into changes in the coverage of search engines over time.

In parallel with HCE investigations, other studies attempted to monitor changes in search engine indexes over time by periodically testing whether sets of sites or pages were indexed. For instance, an investigation into whether AltaVista, HotBot or Yahoo! (deriving its results from Google) indexed the home pages of 1000 active UK websites from www.a.co.uk to www.zzzz.co.uk over a period of seven months found the results to be remarkably static, but with occasional jumps in the number indexed (Figure 7.2). In the case of Google the jumps were particularly large (Thelwall, 2001). This was attributed to Google's expanding its storage or pruning its index, but it could also have been because of changes in its indexing or reporting algorithms. At about the same time, non-researchers coined the term 'Google dance' for short periods of time each month when Google's results fluctuated. This seems to have been caused by monthly

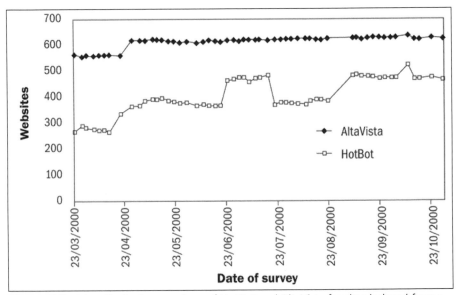

Figure 7.2 *A longitudinal comparison of HotBot and AltaVista for sites indexed from a set of 1000 (Thelwall, 2001)*

updates of Google's index being slowly rolled out to its servers around the world (see www.google-dance-tool.com for an illustration). Moreover, search engine website or page coverage research seems to have stopped in 2001, and so little is known about fluctuations in results over time for current search engines.

A different approach to investigating changes over time is to pick a specific topic and analyse changes in the results reported. Bar-Ilan picked the topic Informetrics and periodically harvested the results returned for the query *informetrics OR informetric* (or equivalent) from June 1998 to 2006 in a variety of popular search engines (Bar-Ilan, 2000; Bar-Ilan and Peritz, 2004, 2008). She used a computer program to extract a list of matching URLs from the results and compared the lists produced on different dates. She concluded that, whilst the number of matches expanded over time, search engines appeared to temporarily or permanently forget pages in the sense of not returning them for a relevant search even though they had been previously returned, still existed and still matched the search. This forgetfulness resulted in lost information because, although some forgotten pages contained information replicated in returned pages, other forgotten pages did not. Further investigations revealed cases where a search engine had indexed pages but did not return them for relevant matches. These findings were corroborated by similar research that planted specific rare terms in web pages and periodically tested whether the pages were returned for relevant queries (Mettrop and Nieuwenhuysen, 2001). In conclusion, the lost information is worrying from the perspective of searchers, and the findings hint at the complexity of search engine algorithms.

In terms of good avenues for new research, all of the above types of study need to be replicated in order to identify any significant differences. It would also be interesting to apply the same methods to the wide range of search services currently on the web, including those popular in different countries or specializing in blogs or other web genres. A good study should find out as much as possible about any differences and investigate possible reasons for them. Finally, the issue of how frequently a search engine updates its index is important and there is scope for research into this, such as by monitoring changes in the indexing of a defined set of pages (Lewandowski, Wahlig and Meyer-Bautor, 2006).

Internal consistency

In addition to fluctuations over time, search engine results can be internally inconsistent in the sense of being apparently illogical (Smith, 1999; Snyder and Rosenbaum, 1999). One way this can manifest itself is through giving more results when a query is refined than for the original query. For instance the query *dog cat* ought to give fewer results than *dog* alone or *cat* alone because pages matching *dog cat* ought to contain both terms. For some pairs of words this is not always true, however. Although such Boolean inconsistency has not been extensively investigated, another source of inconsistency has: changes in HCEs between different results pages for the same query.

The search engine Bing has been investigated for the extent to which its HCEs change on different pages of results (Thelwall, 2008a). The experiment submitted 4000 single-word queries extracted from a blog data source, recording Bing's HCE on each results page and downloading all available results pages. The findings revealed a curious pattern. For searches giving an initial HCE under 300 or over 16,000, the HCEs tended not to change between results pages. In the range of 300–16,000 for the initial results page HCE, however, the HCE on the last results page tended to be about half of the HCE on the first results page. This change was attributed to Bing's automatic results filtering. Search engines are known to filter results so as to avoid returning too many pages from the same website and pages that are too similar to previously returned pages (Dean and Henzinger, 2000). This filtering process is resource intensive and so it seems reasonable for search engines not to do it for the entire results set at once but only for a fraction of the results, including those to be returned for a particular page. If this is correct, then additional filtering would reduce the total number of available results, explaining the reducing HCEs. For searches with high initial HCEs the filtering for the full 1000 matches returned may be such a small proportion of the available results as to leave the HCE unchanged. In contrast, for searches with low initial HCEs, it could be that all filtering is complete before the first results page is returned, explaining the consistent behaviour outside the 250–16,000 range. A corollary is that low HCEs tend to represent matching URLs after filtering, whereas high HCEs tend to represent the total number of matching URLs without any filtering (Thelwall, 2008a, 2008b).

Whilst the above research focused on single-word queries, with the implicit assumption that different queries were likely to have similar behaviours, Uyar (2009b) showed that this was not true. He found that the number of words in a query had a significant impact on the difference between the initial HCE and the number of results returned, with multiple-word queries producing bigger differences (Uyar, 2009b). The experiment used only queries with an initial HCE of between 1 and 1000 and its focus was on the appearance of accuracy in the results when a search engine promised one number of results with the HCE on the first page of results and then delivered a different total number of results.

A study with a wider scope compared different search engines' HCEs for the same queries. Whilst not directly assessing internal consistency, the differences may shed light on the workings of individual search engines, and the study included some statistics about the internal workings of search engines (Thelwall,

2008b). For instance, the HCEs of Google and Yahoo! were five to six times larger than those of Bing (then called Live Search). The paper also produced various graphs to illustrate the complex relationships between HCEs and the number of URLs returned for the three search engines. Figure 7.3 illustrates the number of URLs, websites and top-level domains (TLDs) returned for queries against their initial HCEs, showing that the pattern is not straightforward and there are many anomalies (isolated dots on the graph indicating unusual results).

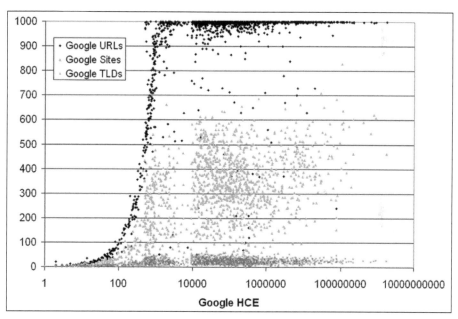

Figure 7.3 Comparison of URLs, websites and TLDs against HCEs for Google (logarithmic x-axis scale) (Thelwall, 2008b)

A more complex study investigated the terms in a document that were apparently indexed, from the perspective of stemming (Uyar, 2009a). It compared the difference in results between queries for singular and plural words, for combined words and for verbs with various postfixes. One of the tests examined the extent to which queries for singular word forms would be matched against documents containing equivalent plural word forms. The results suggested that stemming policies were widely used by search engines but that they varied between documents rather than being generic.

There is a lot of scope for future similar research. In addition to investigations of other major search engines, including non-standard search engines like blog or news search engines, investigations of other types of search, such as phrase searches, link searches or other advanced searches, seem particularly promising. Such experiments need access to an appropriate search engine applications programming interface (API) to automatically submit searches and process the results if they are to be conducted on a large scale. This is available to non-programmers in the LexiURL Searcher software (lexiurl.wlv.ac.uk) for Bing and Yahoo! This used to be possible for Google too, but it now offers an Ajax interface rather than a traditional API.

Search engine bias

A few studies have attempted to identify international biases in search engine indexes. Since search engines are important gateways to the web, any international biases could have commercial repercussions for countries in terms of lost potential online business and this is, therefore, an important issue (Cho and Roy, 2004; Cho, Roy and Adams, 2005; Fortunato et al., 2006). An international comparative experiment assessed bias by taking a systematic sample of websites (with short domain names) from the USA, China, Singapore and Taiwan and used queries to assess whether they were indexed by Google, AltaVista and AllTheWeb. There was clear bias because the USA was better indexed than the rest. The reason for the difference did not seem to be language or deliberate national bias, but simply that countries with older websites were better covered (Vaughan and Thelwall, 2004). This conclusion was reached by counting the number of hyperlinks to each website, which revealed that countries that were poorly represented also received fewer links to their websites. Given that search engines use hyperlinks to find new websites and the number of links to websites tends to grow over time, older websites would have more links to them and hence would be easier to find. Hence countries with older websites, such as early web adopter the USA, would naturally be better indexed. A follow-up study confirmed the above results but also included Yahoo! China, finding that it provided particularly good coverage of China and also of neighbouring countries (Vaughan and Zhang, 2007).

The same multiple-country comparative approach was also used for the Internet Archive (Thelwall and Vaughan, 2004). This is a website that indefinitely archives as much of the web as possible, storing multiple versions of each web page so that changes over time can be investigated. This archive was found to have similar biases to commercial search engines, and for the same reasons.

In terms of future research it would be useful to assess a wider range of countries for biased representation in commercial search engines. Perhaps more urgently, it would be interesting to assess the extent of coverage and bias in search engines that are deliberately biased in the sense of being targeted at a particular language or country. This includes local versions of search engines, like google.co.uk, and national search engines like naver.kr in South Korea. Although this type of research is more recent than the other reviewed studies, it still needs to be extended to a wider range of search engines.

Conclusion

The research reviewed in this chapter takes a webometric rather than an IR approach to evaluating search engines. This helps researchers and other users rather than the search engine designers. The various studies show that although search engines implement algorithms, they are so complex that they can give quite strange results in some respects. The techniques used for evaluation are all mathematically very simple – mostly just simple counting – but are revealing when applied on a large scale to extract patterns, such as those in Figures 8.2 and 8.3. In consequence, most research uses a program to submit queries and record the results. This is possible for Yahoo! and Bing via their APIs.

There is wide scope for new experiments because search engines are under constant development and so it even makes sense periodically to repeat previous research. Moreover, there is room for studies of different search types, such as link searches or document type-specific searches. A good project should probably start with a large-scale study but include follow-up work to diagnose reasons for any patterns and anomalies found.

References

Arasu, A., Cho, J., Garcia-Molina, H., Paepcke, A. and Raghavan, S. (2001) Searching the Web, *ACM Transactions on Internet Technology*, **1** (1), 2–43.

Badue, C., Almeida, J., Almeida, V., Baeza-Yates, R., Ribeiro-Neto, B., Ziviani, A. et al. (in press) Capacity Planning for Vertical Search Engines, *Journal of the American Society for Information Science and Technology*, http://arxiv.org/abs/1006.5059.

Bar-Ilan, J. (1999) Search Engine Results Over Time: a case study on search engine stability, *Cybermetrics*, www.cindoc.csic.es/cybermetrics/articles/v2i1p1.html.

Bar-Ilan, J. (2000) The Web as an Information Source on Informetrics? A content analysis. *Journal of American Society for Information Science*, **51** (5), 432–43.

Bar-Ilan, J. (2002) Methods for Measuring Search Engine Performance Over Time, *Journal of the American Society for Information Science and Technology*, **53** (4), 308–19.

Bar-Ilan, J. (2004) The Use of Web Search Engines in Information Science Research, *Annual Review of Information Science and Technology*, **38**, 231–88.

Bar-Ilan, J. and Peritz, B. C. (2004) Evolution, Continuity, and Disappearance of Documents on a Specific Topic on the Web: a longitudinal study of 'informetrics', *Journal of the American Society for Information Science and Technology*, **55** (11), 980–90.

Bar-Ilan, J. and Peritz, B. C. (2008) The Lifespan of 'Informetrics' on the Web: an eight year study (1998–2006), *Scientometrics,* **79** (1), 7–25.

Barroso, L. A., Dean, J. and Holzle, U. (2003) Web Search for a Planet: the Google cluster architecture, *IEEE Micro,* March-April, 22–8.

Bharat, K. and Broder, A. (1998) A Technique for Measuring the Relative Size and Overlap of Public Web Search Engines, *Computer Networks and ISDN Systems,* **30** (1–7), 379–88.

Cho, J. and Roy, S. (2004) Impact of Web Search Engines on Page Popularity, *Proceedings of the World-Wide Web Conference, May 2004* http://oak.cs.ucla.edu/~cho/papers/cho-bias.pdf.

Cho, J., Roy, S. and Adams, R. E. (2005) Page Quality: in search of an unbiased web ranking, *Proceedings of 2005 ACM International Conference on Management of Data (SIGMOD),* http://oak.cs.ucla.edu/~cho/papers/cho-quality-long.pdf.

Dean, J. H. and Henzinger, M. R. (2000) USA Patent No. 6138113.

Ding, W. and Marchionini, G. (1996) A Comparative Study of Web Search Service Performance. In *Proceedings of the 59th Annual Meeting of the American Society for Information Science, Baltimore, MD,* 136–42.

Fortunato, S., Flammini, A., Menczer, F. and Vespignani, A. (2006) Topical Interests and the Mitigation of Search Engine Bias, Proceedings of the National Academy of Sciences of the USA, **103** (34), 12684–9. doi:10.1073/ pnas.0605525103,www.ncbi.nlm.nih.gov/pmc/articles/PMC1568910/.

Järvelin, K. and Kekalainen, J. (2002) Cumulated Gain-based Evaluation of IR Techniques, *ACM Transactions on Information Systems,* **20** (4), 422–46.

Kilgarriff, A. and Grefenstette, G. (2003) Introduction to the Special Issue on the Web as Corpus, *Computational Linguistics,* **29** (3), 333–47.

Lawrence, S. and Giles, C. (1998) Searching the World Wide Web, *Science,* **280** (5360), 98–100.

Lawrence, S. and Giles, C. L. (1999) Accessibility of Information on the Web, *Nature,* **400** (6740), 107–9.

Lewandowski, D. and Mayr, P. (2006) Exploring the Academic Invisible Web, *Library Hi Tech,* **24** (4), 529–39.

Lewandowski, D., Wahlig, H. and Meyer-Bautor, G. (2006) The Freshness of Web Search Engine Databases, *Journal of Information Science,* **32** (2), 131–48.

Mettrop, W. and Nieuwenhuysen, P. (2001) Internet Search Engines: fluctuations in document accessibility, *Journal of Documentation,* **57** (5), 623–51.

Meyer, C., Grabowski, R., Han, H.-Y., Mantzouranis, K. and Moses, S. (2003) The World Wide Web as Linguistic Corpus, *Language and Computers,* **46** (1), 241–54.

Rousseau, R. (1999) Daily Time Series of Common Single Word Searches in AltaVista and NorthernLight, *Cybermetrics,* **2/3,** www.cindoc.csic.es/cybermetrics/articles/v2002i2001p2002.html.

Smith, A. G. (1999) A Tale of Two Web Spaces: comparing sites using web impact factors, *Journal of Documentation,* **55** (5), 577–92.

Snyder, H. W. and Rosenbaum, H. (1999) Can Search Engines Be Used for Web-link Analysis? A critical review, *Journal of Documentation*, **55** (4), 375–84.

Thelwall, M. (2001) The Responsiveness of Search Engine Indexes, *Cybermetrics*, **5** (1), www.cindoc.csic.es/cybermetrics/articles/v5i1p1.html.

Thelwall, M. (2002) Methodologies for Crawler Based Web Surveys, *Internet Research: Electronic Networking and Applications*, **12** (2), 124–38.

Thelwall, M. (2008a) Extracting Accurate and Complete Results from Search Engines: case study Windows Live, *Journal of the American Society for Information Science and Technology*, **59** (1), 38–50.

Thelwall, M. (2008b) Quantitative Comparisons of Search Engine Results, *Journal of the American Society for Information Science and Technology*, **59** (11), 1702–10.

Thelwall, M. and Vaughan, L. (2004) A Fair History of the Web? Examining country balance in the Internet Archive, *Library and Information Science Research*, **26** (2), 162–76.

Thelwall, M., Vaughan, L. and Björneborn, L. (2005) Webometrics, *Annual Review of Information Science and Technology*, **39**, 81–135.

Turpin, A. and Scholer, F. (2006) User Performance versus Precision Measures for Simple Search Tasks. In *Proceedings of the 29th Annual International ACM SIGIR Conference on Research and Development in information Retrieval*, Association for Computer Machinery, 11–18.

Uyar, A. (2009a) Google Stemming Mechanisms, *Journal of Information Science*, **35** (5), 499–514.

Uyar, A. (2009b) Investigation of the Accuracy of Search Engine Hit Counts, *Journal of Information Science*, **35** (4), 469–80.

Van Couvering, E. (2004) New Media? The political economy of internet search engines, paper presented at the Annual Conference of the International Association of Media and Communications Researchers, Porto Alegre, Brazil.

Van Couvering, E. (2007) Is Relevance Relevant? Market, science, and war: discourses of search engine quality, *Journal of Computer-Mediated Communication*, **12** (3), http://jcmc.indiana.edu/vol12/issue13/vancouvering.html.

van Rijsbergen, C. J. (1979) *Information Retrieval*, 2nd edn, Butterworths.

Vaughan, L. and Thelwall, M. (2004) Search Engine Coverage Bias: evidence and possible causes, *Information Processing & Management*, **40** (4), 693–707.

Vaughan, L. and Zhang, Y. (2007) Equal Representation by Search Engines? A comparison of websites across countries and domains, *Journal of Computer-Mediated Communication*, **12** (3), http://jcmc.indiana.edu/vol12/issue3/vaughan.html.

Zaragoza, H., Cambazoglu, B. B. and Baeza-Yates, R. (2010) Web Search Solved? All result rankings the same? *Proceedings of the 19th ACM international conference on Information and knowledge management*, www.hugo-zaragoza.net/academic/pdf/zaragoza_CIKM2010.pdf.

Index